**CCCC STUDIES IN WRITING & RHETORIC**

*Edited by Steve Parks, University of Virginia*

The aim of the CCCC Studies in Writing & Rhetoric (SWR) Series is to influence how we think about language in action and especially how writing gets taught at the college level. The methods of studies vary from the critical to historical to linguistic to ethnographic, and their authors draw on work in various fields that inform composition—including rhetoric, communication, education, discourse analysis, psychology, cultural studies, and literature. Their focuses are similarly diverse—ranging from individual writers and teachers, to work on classrooms and communities and curricula, to analyses of the social, political, and material contexts of writing and its teaching.

SWR was one of the first scholarly book series to focus on the teaching of writing. It was established in 1980 by the Conference on College Composition and Communication (CCCC) in order to promote research in the emerging field of writing studies. As our field has grown, the research sponsored by SWR has continued to articulate the commitment of CCCC to supporting the work of writing teachers as reflective practitioners and intellectuals.

We are eager to identify influential work in writing and rhetoric as it emerges. We thus ask authors to send us project proposals that clearly situate their work in the field and show how they aim to redirect our ongoing conversations about writing and its teaching. Proposals should include an overview of the project, a brief annotated table of contents, and a sample chapter. They should not exceed 10,000 words.

To submit a proposal, please register as an author at www.editorial manager.com/nctebp. Once registered, follow the steps to submit a proposal (be sure to choose SWR Book Proposal from the drop-down list of article submission types).

# BEYOND PROGRESS IN THE PRISON CLASSROOM

## OPTIONS AND OPPORTUNITIES

**Anna Plemons**
*Washington State University*

Conference on College
Composition and
Communication

National Council of
Teachers of English

Staff Editor: Bonny Graham
Manuscript Editor: Ernesto Yermoli
Series Editor: Steve Parks
Interior Design: Mary Rohrer
Cover Design: Pat Mayer
Cover Photo: copyright 2019; Photo by Peter Merts, courtesy of the California Arts
   Council. www.artsincorrections.org

NCTE Stock Number: 34658; eStock Number: 34665
ISBN 978-0-8141-3465-8; eISBN 978-0-8141-3466-5

It is the policy of NCTE in its journals and other publications to provide a forum for the
open discussion of ideas concerning the content and the teaching of English and the language arts. Publicity accorded to any particular point of view does not imply endorsement
by the Executive Committee, the Board of Directors, or the membership at large, except in
announcements of policy, where such endorsement is clearly specified.

NCTE provides equal employment opportunity (EEO) to all staff members and applicants
for employment without regard to race, color, religion, sex, national origin, age, physical,
mental or perceived handicap/disability, sexual orientation including gender identity or expression, ancestry, genetic information, marital status, military status, unfavorable discharge
from military service, pregnancy, citizenship status, personal appearance, matriculation or
political affiliation, or any other protected status under applicable federal, state, and local
laws.

Every effort has been made to provide current URLs and email addresses, but because of the
rapidly changing nature of the web, some sites and addresses may no longer be accessible.

**Library of Congress Cataloging-in-Publication Data**

Names: Plemons, Anna, 1977– author.
Title: Beyond progress in the prison classroom : options and opportunities / Anna Plemons
Description: Urbana, Illinois : National Council of Teachers of English, [2019] | Series:
   CCCC studies in writing & rhetoric | Includes bibliographical references and index. |
   Summary: "Explores how prison writing programs still make use of colonial ways of
   knowing and being that work against the decolonial intentions of the field, and suggests
   indigenous scholarship as a theoretical basis for pushing back against individualized,
   ecomonic assessments of value and designing principles for research and pedagogy that
   are respectful, reciprocal, and relational"—Provided by publisher.
Identifiers: LCCN 2019025741 (print) | LCCN 2019025742 (ebook) | ISBN
   9780814134658 (trade paperback) | ISBN 9780814134665 (adobe pdf)
Subjects: LCSH: Prisoners—Education—United States. | Creative writing—Study and
   teaching—United States. | Writing centers. | Prisoners' writings, American. | Indigenous
   peoples—Research—Methodology.
Classification: LCC HV8883.3.U5 P54 2019 (print) | LCC HV8883.3.U5 (ebook) |
   DDC 365/.6660973—dc23
LC record available at https://lccn.loc.gov/2019025741
LC ebook record available at https://lccn.loc.gov/2019025742

# CONTENTS

# FOREWORD

ANNA AND I HAVE A HISTORY of intellectual camaraderie, wrapped up in hallway and office conversations about race, our families, the landscape of Eastern Washington, a love of colorful earrings and scarves, and quandaries over how to ethically engage in research activities around the public work of composition. Our first formal foray into sharing our institutional and ethical entanglements was in a CCCC 2013 panel. At that time, I was struggling to reconcile how I had allowed my pretenure academic life to draw me into a space where I felt as though it were my job to use the stories and lives of Indigenous women as commodities to be traded in the scholarly publishing game. As an Anishinaabekwe,[1] this was not who I was taught to be. (I've since been on a long slow journey to rearticulate my relations.)

Meanwhile, Anna, who had been working in the Arts in Corrections program at New Folsom Prison, was grappling with her desire to ethically share the stories of incarcerated writers and teachers so as to problematize our savior narratives around the public work of composition. And yet, her entanglements with university IRB processes were making clear that in spite of her goals to lift the voices of these writers and teachers, her job working within an IRB structure was to adhere to a "disciplining structure whose primary intention is not support of sound, ethical research, but rather, the health and safety of the institution." In short, we both found ourselves embroiled in and pulled into complicity with institutional structures that were not built by and for marginalized folks.

We both knew it shouldn't have to be this way. We grappled. We sat still. We reflected. We listened. We wrote.

Fast-forward through Anna finishing a PhD, continuing to work at the prison and in the university, and drafting this book. What you see in these pages is Anna's slow and thoughtful processing of what it means to reconsider our work as compositionists who exist in often oppressive, and always slow-moving, institutional structures. Part of this work is to reposition our understanding of how the system works in the first place. To that end, Anna engages with a model of relationality shared by Indigenous thinkers.

And here feels like the place to out her (but trust me, she will, too): Anna is a white woman. She's a white woman who has, for years, been slowly thinking through whether it's even ethical for her to share the ways theories of relationality have helped her see outside a colonial perspective. She's been careful in this work, at times overly apologetic—always worried about "we" versus "I." And now, because she couldn't draft forever, you see where her thinking is at today.

Part of the work of relationality is to be transparent about our entanglements in institutional structures, in part because, as Linda Hogan says, "we are co-creators in the universe, the world, within all the rest, all fluid, shifting movement, and without the emphasis on measurement. The world is there in its entirety, not in segments" (Cordova ix). Being honest that we are in relation with, and co-create, these institutions, we are then called to be honest about our lived embodied being in the world. But we are also called to not stand still. Not standing still means engaging outside of our bubbles. Acknowledging ALL our relations, not just the ones we like to hang out with at conferences.

And that, perhaps, is what is most exciting to me about this project: it offers a model for engaging with Indigenous thought to think through problems that may or may not include Indigenous peoples. In doing so, Anna forces the question: Is it okay to use Indigenous theory to talk about groups other than Indigenous folks? At the end of this book, Anna, Steve, and I grapple with some of these issues. I am firmly of the belief that it *is* okay, so long as it's done with care. To not engage is erasure. Yet, my mind may shift with time. As it does. As it should.

Along with directly providing a model for working with Indigenous thought, Anna's work also reflects deeply on the trope of writing as liberation, which white liberals tend to take up in highly problematic ways. Anna says here something she told me long ago and that has always resonated with me: "I often say to students—and here I am speaking also to myself—that in prison work and on campus, it is important to 'beware the helpers.'" Beware those who march into prisons with pens in hand, ready to save the prisoners from themselves (all the while collecting savior stories of transformation to trade on the academic market). Beware those who preach community engagement, but spend more time presenting at conferences about their community work than actually in the communities themselves. Beware the writing teachers who, with good intentions, believe they are saving students through what they see as progressive pedagogies.

I can't not think of Asao Inoue's 2019 CCCC keynote address when thinking about Anna's work. Inoue asks, in refrain, "How do we language so people stop killing each other?" ("How Do We"). Anna's work offers a model that shows, through relationality, how the line between prisons and universities—between prisoners and teachers and students—is blurry. "[M]any of us can acknowledge White language supremacy as the status quo in our classrooms and society," Inoue says, "but not see all of it, and so perpetuate it." What Anna is trying to get us to see is that white language supremacy is built into the very fabric of our institutions and our intentions—we cannot ignore it. It exists always already in relation to the work we do, so we need to account for it, face it, and find ways of being and doing that language differently.

And so, I leave you with Anna's words—a questioning, a reflection on what it means to be a well-meaning white teacher-scholar in a predominantly white field who sees the structure for what it is, who knows it's profoundly messed up, who sees possibilities, and who wants to rethink the work of composition. She comes to you with a good heart.

Miigwetch/Thanks,
Kristin L. Arola

## PREFACE

I GAVE A COMPLETED FIRST DRAFT of this manuscript to Marty Williams, the incarcerated teaching artist whose story is interwoven here with my own. I would have also liked to have shown it to Spoon Jackson, the other incarcerated teaching artist important to this project. However, by the time I had completed it, Spoon had been moved without notice down to a Level Three institution in Southern California, leaving the crowd of pigeons that he used to feed through the chain link between the sally port and the small side yard shuffling around, hungrily pecking at the concrete. The chaotic and transitory California prison is, by design, at odds with the relational methodology I point toward in this book. My inability to discuss the finished text with Spoon frustrates the end to my own small story.

Although I did not get to officially say good-bye to Spoon, I did have a chance to say good-bye to Marty the day before he was slated to leave New Folsom. We stood, shoulder to shoulder, facing the same blank wall, speaking in hushed tones and couched terms about the blessing of working together over some five years. As it turns out, it would be another year before he was actually transferred to a Level Three prison, so I continued to see him in class. We continued to have conversations about teaching and writing in prison. And since we had already said good-bye, we fell back into the practice of shaking hands at the end of class and chatting our way out of the library door that opens onto the sally port. Marty would wait for a guard to let him back onto the yard that bridges the sally port and his housing unit and I would turn and walk the other way, without looking back, down the windowless hallway of the Medical Clinic where inmates wait on narrow wooden benches for pill dispensation.

This space between saying good-bye to Marty and his transfer a year later afforded me some extra time to learn from Marty, a self-made scholar of the highest degree. The breadth of his knowledge and his careful application of it had earned him the title of "Mad Monk" among his incarcerated colleagues. I was hopeful yet nervous when I handed him the first draft of this book. I did not presume that he would want to wade through the prose of a novice scholar trying to find her voice, and I wasn't sure that what I had written reflected and was respectful of the community of writers at New Folsom.

A month after giving Marty the draft we sat down together in the damp and windowless prison library to discuss it. I was touched to learn that he had read it through three times and scribbled in the margins. And I knew that he had heard me when he quoted Thoreau: "If I knew for a certainty that a man was coming to my house with the conscious design of doing me good, I should run for my life." I laughed. As is usually the case, what I had wanted to say had already been said long ago in a sentence or two. Thoreau, invited to the conversation, gets at the heart of the issue I have attempted to lay out in this book. There *is* a fundamental problem with conscious designs intended to enact good upon another in his or her own house—and maybe even a deeper violence when the recipients of such good are forced to live somewhere other than their home.

I am grateful to Marty for bringing Thoreau into the conversation, just as I am grateful for his contributions before and after that meeting in the library. I am also grateful for the writers who took up the mantle of Arts in Corrections (AIC) leadership after Spoon and Marty were finally transferred. The shape of the program, and my role in it, has shifted in the intervening years, and many participants who came and went have left their mark on the program and the ideas in this text.

Harry Grant, whose writing inspired both raucous laughter and knowing silence among his peers, told me once that writing was the third parent and fourth child in my family. This idea that the texts we create are members of our family has informed my understanding of the fundamental relatedness of things. And when Jacob

Allen wrote about the guy who frantically ate the petals off the rose bush outside the watch office, the relational threads of life inside came into even clearer focus. The insights of this book would not have been possible without the insights of teachers like Marty and Spoon or writers such as Harry and Jacob. For that reason, this book moves back and forth between academic chapters and narratives from incarcerated students and teachers. My intent is to tell a fuller story about the life of AIC at New Folsom and the relational work that so deeply defines and sustains it.

This book is meant to demonstrate that we can learn from disciplinary language and personal stories and to show, as much as possible, the relationships and community out of which this project emerged.

## ACKNOWLEDGMENTS

THIS BOOK OWES ITS LIFE TO A great many people. First, I want to thank the community of incarcerated writers at New Folsom Prison who welcomed me into their classrooms and have let me return again and again over the last decade. It has been my honor to be present for the birth of so many stories, some of which appear in this book.

And to Carol Hinds, who has been a fierce and tireless advocate for Arts in Corrections and who has shared her own story with grace and power. You speak life into the hearts of many, and I am so glad to join the host of those who are buoyed by your care and kindness.

To the constellation of folks, including Jim Carlson, who inhabit the past and future of the California Arts in Corrections Program, I express my gratitude. With vision and fortitude, you made Arts in Corrections what it was, and with some fancy bureaucratic dancing, a few of you even found ways to keep the lights on during the dark years. Thanks in large part to the steady leadership of Laurie Brooks at the William James Association and Alma Robinson at California Lawyers for the Arts, funding for Arts in Corrections has returned to prisons across the state. I am a benefactor of your resolve to make a way when it seemed there was none.

Likewise, many administrators and staff at New Folsom have overseen my coming and going from the prison. Without good folks like these, who say yes even when it creates extra work, there is no way inside. To Kari Zamora, Therese Giannelli, Dr. Dale Hamad, a succession of supportive wardens, and the custody staff who have worked with Arts in Corrections over the years to ensure that classes happen, I offer thanks.

I also want to thank Peter Merts for his contribution to this book and the California Arts Council for permission to include

Copyright 2019. Photo by Peter Merts, courtesy of the California Arts Council.
www.artsincorrections.org

Peter's work. Peter, you have opened a beautiful and humanizing window into so many Arts in Corrections classrooms, and I know I am not alone in being grateful for the light and life you have documented with your photographs.

I would also like to recognize my faculty mentors and the colleagues who have provided strong support and helpful critique as this book has taken shape. To Robert Eddy, who first suggested that I could be a scholar. And to Victor Villanueva, Kristin Arola, and Patty Ericsson, who shepherded me down that path, each generously giving of their time and expertise. And to my colleagues near and far—Beth Buyserie, Tobi Jacobi, Laura Rogers, Patrick Berry, Rebecca Ginsburg, Maggie Shelledy, and Tabitha Espina—thank you for sharpening my thinking about the (im)possibilities of teaching and learning in prison and for sharing your time with me.

I am deeply grateful to Steve Parks for believing this book should be born and for his vision, patience, and keen insight throughout the process. Additionally, to the anonymous SWR reviewers, who generously offered their time and honest feedback. It was both humbling and energizing to have you speak back to the ideas I had put down on paper. The text is stronger for your contributions, and I thank you. A special thanks, also, to Bonny Graham and Ernesto Yermoli at NCTE for your work in preparing this book for publication.

To my mom and dad, I offer thanks. You have woven Arts in Corrections into your life, sharing your home and your hearts with so many teaching artists over the years. Your example inspires me. I know that I stand on your shoulders, and I don't take for granted that the rich experiences and open doors that have marked my life are some of your many gifts to me.

To Sarah, Moses, and Josephine—you have shown both grace and interest as you have shared your life with this work. I will never forget when you repurposed a recycled version of my dissertation into a paper chain to decorate our house for my birthday. In that moment, as in many others, I was grateful for the ways that the seemingly desperate spheres of home and work have pieced together into an imperfect but beautiful whole.

And to Jason, with whom I have walked, hand in hand, nearly twenty years. You see the best in me, and I hope I have carried that sacred gift forward into all the classrooms where I teach. It has been the joy of my life to dream, risk, and build alongside you. You have my heart.

## Eulogy 2

Squat monoliths stare unmoving
Beneath the rolling gray,
The b-ball courts dark with last nights
rain.
Steel mouths gape and spew humanity
Into a shallow basin
To endlessly walk a warped asphalt
track
Around and around and around
Like Ixion to the wheel
Like clockwork gears, like a snake
Devouring itself.
And on the dark courts dark men
Spit and bark
Into a brother's face
While white men crowd a short wood
bench
To flay a friend, to skin him alive,
While brown and red skins
And yellow skins slap blue balls
Against the monolithic face
That stares at them all
Close-mouthed.

And one might have been born
To an old pale prison,
To old pale prisons
Of handhewn granite bone

Full of faces, full of ghosts,
Full of straight black bars,
To the jangle of keys
To the night cries
To where only the fittest survive
And there's never a question
Of where you are at
And then one day
It's squat monoliths
And a big warped wheel
And somebody stands among
the orbiting flesh and says
*Where are we going?*

—Martin Williams

## All I Can Do Is Words

"YOU HAVE 60 SECONDS LEFT ON THIS CALL" declares the automated female voice, taking hostage a conversation that cannot possibly be wrapped up in 60 seconds but will be cut off regardless.

"Sorry about that. What were you saying?" I ask the helpful stranger on the other end of the line while trying to pretend I'm not hiding anything and I'm just a normal human being deserving of normal information. She continues with a professionalism that makes me wonder if she knows what the countdown means, or if she just isn't one to lose focus on distractions.

"Your father is post-op and recovering from surgically administered shocks to his heart in an attempt to steady his arrhythmia. His BPM is currently 160 and the cardiologists aren't sure why. The doctors are ready to discharge him as soon as his resting heart rate steadies." I'm scared my Dad might be leaving us, and not because of his ailing body. I want to know if he is losing his mind.

"How come he doesn't know who I am?" "THIS CALL IS BEING MONITORED AND RECORDED." This overpowering statement of dominance cannot be muted, talked over, or ignored as it screams in our ears, and in my mind hear a few more of our allotted seconds tick away. I want to smash the phone against the wall and scream as the flat voice reminds me that even at my most vulnerable I must be watched and guarded. I want to punch myself in the face for making this so. Instead I sit in my embarrassment, listening to my healthy heart as it pounds in my ears.

"Your father is on a lot of medication and still recovering from anesthesia." The nurse continues on unruffled and I imagine her calm and composed in a high-stress emergency room. Her proficient demeanor reassures me that my father is in good hands, but at the same time I'm uncomfortably aware that she has to know why this call is timed and recorded. "He'll be out of it for a while, but should be fine when—" "YOU HAVE 30 SECONDS LEFT ON THIS CALL." Three more seconds tick by during the unavoidable interruption from the heartless bitch who is always in the background, ready and waiting to hijack this call. My mind is racing.

Will we be able to wrap this up in 27 seconds or will it help if I can call back is there anyone after me on the phone sign-up list my dad being in the hospital has to be a good enough excuse to double-dial and if someone's got a problem with it I don't give a fuck right now but would my dad be mad at me if I got into a fight over trying to call him and what if he dies and I'm in the hole what good is another phone call I hate myself so much right now am I going to be able to talk to my dad again?

"I'm sorry about that, what were you saying?" I ask shamefully, picturing the nurse's sympathetic eyes staring at my old broken dad while she judges me for all the stress I've added to his life and blames me for contributing to his health problems and for not being there in person to help take care of him.

"He should be fine when the anesthesia wears off." Her smooth recovery makes me wonder if she's dealt with these types of calls before. "He fainted and fell on his head then drove himself to a hospital and was rushed here because we are a specialized facility. He's been operated on and we're continuing to monitor his vitals until they become steady and an accurate diagnosis can be made."

I'm trying to take this all in, trying to figure out what I can do, trying to figure out who I can call, how I can act, how I should respond to be there for my fading father. It doesn't matter. I can't do anything or be anywhere for anyone.

She has a kind voice wrapped in sharp competence that makes me feel like I've been both hugged and slapped as the supportive sound punches through my anger and self-pity.

"Excuse me?" I reply. So she asks again earnestly, with the professionalism of protocol and the sincere assumption that there exists a level of normalcy in my life that would allow me to be the one able to offer help to my father when he needs it the most. "Can I please get your contact information?"

My voice gives out on me as I'm forced to say out loud what I thought had been so obvious.

"I'm sorry, I'm in prison."

—Bryson L. Cole

**Showing Up**

It is ten minutes by car from Karen's Bakery to the front gate of the prison across the river, through the false-front row of Wild West trinketeers, antique dealers, and upscale coffee houses. Past the park, senior center, and City Hall, left onto Prison Road with signs every 50 feet: "NO STOPPING OR TURNING." Old oaks stand mighty and quiet. Golden leaves loosened by the breeze spin in the air and take their time falling. The roll of the hill hides what lies on the other side; for about half a mile I can pretend I am in a state park or animal sanctuary. The deer step carefully to the main gate where the green grass grows thick around a steam vent. A first-rate prison requires acres of undeveloped space, and this land was purchased cheap, long before suburbanites decided to live in the area. Represa, California, land once belonging to the Maidu, now houses over 5,000 incarcerated people, none of whom are allowed to vote.

It's smiles and small talk while I wait for my gate pass. The "Boys from Minimum"—grown men with beards and aging mothers—keep their eyes down as they meticulously shape shrubs and water marigolds. Once inside, it's a quarter-mile walk to the A/B gate metal detector and two flimsy guardhouses that remind me of the leaky portable classrooms of my high school. A river rock weighs down the pages of the sign-in book. I move it slightly to add my name, then hold up the back of my hand for the rubber stamp and watch as the ink run through the fissures on dry skin. "Remember, California does not honor hostage negotiations," says the guard as he hands back my ID. I laugh, follow the script. The tower guard releases the lock. I close the heavy door behind me.

There are no more marigolds. Lines of dark moss and piles of bird poop sparingly break up the gray of the concrete. A clinician, dressed for business, pushes in behind me, scurrying toward the flat face of A Facility with a manila folder held over her head. "Damn seagulls," she grunts, chopping her sensible heels against the uneven concrete, a crate of files bumping beside her on small plastic wheels. I hadn't noticed the gulls dipping behind the wall, circling, their short cries muffled by the echo and din around me: metal scraping metal, human voices, keys, leather, fans and hissing steam. I imagine the ocean. It is far away. Here, seagulls are a sign of garbage, crowding. They drop gooey turds on hot pavement—reminders that no one here is on vacation.

It is a five-minute walk to C Facility. The road is straight. I think about class. To my right is the exterior wall of a housing block—a squat, scarred giant with rusty tears seeping from eight-inch slits of dark glass, one eye for each cell. The giant looks out, without interest, over a twenty-foot, two-ply electric fence, whipstitched with concertina. The hand with my gate pass and ID is cold in my pocket. On the fence, at eye level, a black-and-white sign shows a falling stick figure, lightning bolts at his feet: "*PELIGRO.*"

I enter C Facility behind four officers and their cuffed charges. As my eyes adjust to the dark, I show my ID for a third time. The floor of the guardroom is raised, so I stare at the guard's belt-buckle while she looks at my license. On the way out, her replacement will ask me why the hell someone from Washington would want to come all this way. I will imagine acting surprised and saying something clever about already having been to Pier 39, but instead I will say nothing.

The fluorescent hallway between the guardroom and the sally port is lined with medical cubicles—large windows, small examining room. I avert my eyes in a reflective act of privacy as I pass the cells reserved for inmates on suicide watch. A guy who came to class once mops the floor. We say hello without shaking hands.

Spoon is sitting on an upturned milk crate outside the AIC classroom, face turned toward the small side yard and the pigeons who wait for him, stretching their necks through the chain link, blinking down the bread crumbs he spreads for them. Spoon is from the Mojave and feels a deep need for open space. Come November, the Blacks and Northern Mexicans will be locked down for one full calendar year, only leaving their cells for twice-weekly showers. The pigeons will continue to come the first two months. Everyone will be hungry.

I set down my bag. I am the guest teacher for the Tuesday poetry class that Spoon teaches. We choose a topic and begin to brainstorm. I shake a stub of chalk between my cupped hands as I wait for the thawing of defenses and the warming of the words that will fill the chalkboard. My fidgeting reminds me of the song I learned in Brownies that makes no sense and strikes me now as part of the landscape of unexamined White privilege that was my childhood: *I'm shaking up my baby bumblebee/Won't my mommy be so proud of me.* One of the new writers points out the line of chalk dust on my slacks. After three hours I will go out the way I came in, but while I am here, we will write from deep wells, some recently discovered under the concrete strewn with broken glass and bits of bone.

Years will pass while I try to write about why incarcerated men and women need to have significant say in how they use the writing classroom space. While I grapple with the lingering colonial sensibility of a profession that hungers for narratives of transformation, the AIC program will be defunded and the incarcerated teachers will be transferred to other institutions; new classes with new writers will begin, and we will all hold our breath for a moment before meeting to show our respect for the ghosts of those who have moved on, whether by force or by choice, from this place where we write with terrifying honesty stories both real and imagined.

In those same two years, a community of writers will form in A Facility. They will begin working on a book. A man who was padlocked into a padded suit the first time I met him will write his way out of solitary and into a class where he can sit in a chair instead of a cage. Men will come and go. For some, writing will be life-saving. For others it will be a diversion. For most, the experience of writing in community will fall somewhere between fully transformative and merely entertaining. And because I, like all the other writing teachers taking their satchels into the prison, will have little real power to determine the direction of each writer's experience my focus will not be on justifying my place as teacher/transformer but on doing my part to make the classroom generative, safe. I will come with paperback books to leave and reams of photocopied passages that I think may speak to the writers. Sometimes I will stand at the chalkboard and sometimes I will sit quietly while writers stand to embrace one another or speak encouragement into the raw silence that follows a reading. But whether I play the role of chalkboard scribbler or silent witness, I will only ever be a guest—invited to listen, not to fix or save.

As I walk both from the front gate to the classroom at New Folsom and from my house to the college campus where I teach, I will think about the prison. And how it is a nearly totalizing place. And how sometimes incarcerated writers add their CDCR numbers to the top right-hand corner of the page, either before or after their names. As I walk and as I read the work of other prison scholars, I will attempt to separate the value of the prison classroom from a practice of trafficking in transformational narratives—not because they are missing, but because they are so powerfully tempting to we teachers who want to know that what we are doing is doing something.

—Anna Plemons

# 1

## Getting Inside: Measuring Something Other Than Progress

> The stories we tell each other tell us who we are, locate us in time and space and history and land, and suggest who gets to speak and how.
>
> —Lisa King, Rose Gubele, and Joyce Rain Anderson,
> *Survivance, Sovereignty, and Story*

> We differ in the presentation of theory, not in our capacity to theorize.
>
> —Lee Maracle, *Oratory: Coming to Theory*

> Absent altered ways of coming to know, making meaning, and acting, we seemed doomed to loop endlessly and helplessly through the same tired actions and reactions, claims and counterclaims, raising the same questions over and over and moving restlessly away from them before we've lived and lain with them.
>
> —Frankie Condon, *Hope I Join the Band*

SYSTEMS OF IMPRISONMENT ARE dehumanizing by design. Because humans are not meant to live in cages, the carceral enterprise requires both prisoner and guard to ignore the relational threads (land, community, family, etc.) that connect us. "This place is about isolation," says incarcerated teaching artist Marty Williams in *At Night I Fly*, a 2011 Swedish documentary about the AIC at New Folsom (Wenzer). "It is about closure of the heart and the mind and the spirit. And the worst thing about this place is that it is what it is. It's doing its job, which is to keep us contained. That's it. It serves no other purpose but containment." The material conditions of incarceration that Williams describes work against the liberatory aims of education that motivate teachers and students alike. These conditions also lead teachers and students who work in carceral spaces to struggle with the tension between complicity and confrontation inherent in such systems—a tension that, although ultimately unresolvable, can be instructive.

Prison classrooms highlight the gap between intention and practice in teaching and make plain the need to pursue decolonial work that does more than revise or amend the ideological underpinnings of the discipline—what Angela Davis calls "pivot[ting] the center" (*Freedom* 145). The central colonialistic ideology that we hoped to have left behind—namely, an obsession with transforming the moral and intellectual deficits of the Other and the use of economic rhetoric in that pursuit—still shows itself quite clearly in the discourse on prison education (as will be discussed later in this chapter). Like Ellen Cushman, I see that emancipatory projects in composition often "fall short of their social justice goals because they critique a content or place of practice without revealing and altering their own structuring tenets" ("Translingual" 239). And it is not only the overtly emancipatory projects that miss the mark. Nuanced iterations of this same ideology still permeate, and therefore hobble, the broader work in composition.

The work of "revealing and altering [our] structural tenets" requires the best efforts of scholars and teachers entering the conversation from as many points and perspectives as possible. With this book, I aim to help disrupt the colonial impulse that uses individual narratives of transformation to measure the efficacy and value of prison education programs. In *Right to Be Hostile*, Erica Meiners offers a sample from the genre: "I was born; I had problems; I made the wrong choices; I was apprehended by the police; I was incarcerated; I found God [or writing] and He [or it] helped me. And . . . my life is now on a better track" (139). The primary problem with transformational narratives is that they focus on the individual and his or her criminal act rather than the wider political and economic landscape. Individual prison narratives of transformation offer evidence for Mignolo's claim that "the rhetoric of modernity is a rhetoric of salvation." Terms like *conversion* have been replaced with words like *development,* but the essential idea—that the object of the colonizer's gaze needs to be transformed—remains (xxiv).

When we de-emphasize individual narratives, our attention can widen to include the relational webs within which we all exist. Consider, for example, the work of Bryson, an incarcerated writer at New Folsom who has been part of an Arts in Corrections (AIC) writer's workshop since 2013. Over the last four years, Bryson's writing has become increasingly clear and poignant. Recently, he wrote a beautiful essay about his father that focused on a hotel where his father had worked as a young man. In the essay, Bryson shares his hope of someday visiting the hotel with his father while also admitting that his father will likely die while he is still in prison. It is impossible to appreciate this work without taking into account the relational webs of family and place that Bryson inhabits.

The class conversation around the first draft of Bryson's essay was intense, personal, and tearful at times. Bryson received helpful feedback from his classmates and was able to spend some time further unpacking his motivation and intention for the piece. The

Photo by Peter Merts.

writers at New Folsom do not have internet access, so I chose to support Bryson's work by printing out the Wikipedia entry of the hotel in the essay. What Bryson needed as a writer was not my expertise, editing, or encouragement, but rather more access to information about something that he had articulated was important to him.

Showing my support for Bryson by using Wikipedia hardly constitutes an educational victory story—and that is precisely why I tell it here. It is the story of a small moment bound up in a larger, relationally complex one. No accurate conversation about Bryson's writing can be had without accounting for the aging of his father; his recent marriage, which grew out of a deeply introspective correspondence; or the legislative changes in California that give Bryson hope—for the first time—that he might parole. Nor can the story of Bryson's writing practice be told without acknowledging the trust and respect that Bryson shares with his fellow writers and the way that those relationships facilitate personal observations, pointed critique, and genuine laughter, often across racial lines.

The textured, human reality of Bryson's writing practice complicates the value of a focus on individual transformational narratives. It also calls into question the effectiveness of using such narratives as "evidence" that prison education programs are worth their cost to taxpayers. Nonetheless, this kind of economic rhetoric continues to be the coin of the realm in prison programming, as seen in a recent RAND report on prison education full of talk about judicious use of taxpayer dollars, "difficult budgetary times," and the importance of "making science a priority" (Davis et al. iii). The RAND report openly commodifies incarcerated students, emphasizing the importance of delivering a return on investment. The report does not, and really cannot, account for the role that love, or the looming mortality of an elder, or the changing political climate can have on the sagacious use of taxpayer money. Nor does it attempt to account for the ways that race, class, gender, and sexuality overly determine our relationships with and within the US prison system.

As V. F. Cordova points out, "present actions are like layers of snow added to a snowball—the shape of the present outer layer determines the future shape of the whole" (175). This truth—that imminent forms are shaped by current ones—informs my concerns about the direction of prison education programs. If prison education remains shaped by economic logics and a voyeuristic obsession with narratives of transformation, it will continue to reflect the neoliberal policies of the era that oversaw its exponential growth.

Writing about translingualism in *College English,* Cushman asks "scholars and teachers to consider seriously what methodological and pedagogical possibilities for decolonizing knowledge" might be available ("Translingual" 234). I read Cushman's question as a serious invitation to critically assess all the available means for decolonizing knowledge, particularly those that are not yet fully recognized or respected. The AIC program at New Folsom is the context in which I have come to understand Cushman's critique, and also one site where I see promising possibilities for learning from decolonial insights that respect the relational reality of writing.

I want to offer some preliminary definitions as a way to connect this text to the important body of scholarship on decoloniality. The term *decoloniality* means opposition to *coloniality,* a term that I use here to signify the systems of knowledge and attendant socioeconomic structures that elevate certain groups while also purposefully disenfranchising others (Grosfoguel; Mignolo; Ndlovu-Gatsheni and Zondi). Angela Haas suggests that work grounded in decolonial theory examines how both individuals and groups have been affected by and been complicit in colonial legacies. It asks questions that challenge Western knowledge systems, allowing scholars to consider how the "effects and complicities of historical and contemporary colonialism influence research and educational institutions, theories, methodologies, methods, and scholarship" and play out in our "everyday embodied practices" ("Toward" 191). It is these last two projects—recognizing the influence of lingering structures of coloniality on educational research and practice and their quiet influence on daily life—that inform much of the work discussed in this book.

I use *relationality* in this text to mean the claim from Indigenous thought that all things are related.[1] This is much more than a set of guidelines for how to create and sustain good relationships: it is the ontological understanding that "relationships do not merely shape reality, they are reality" (S. Wilson 7). If the relatedness of all things is a fundamental truth that describes a world where humans live in relationship to everything—those who have come before us, those who will follow, the land, the water, and all other animate and inanimate beings—then even non-Indigenous people are responsible to those relations. The philosophical drivers of Western thought have abstracted and obscured this fundamental relatedness (e.g., through Cartesian dualism). Such sustained abstraction has led to the common assumption that relationships are isolatable things that we can take up and just as easily leave behind. Indigenous theory challenges the conception of relationships as a matter of choice, asking scholar-practitioners to reexamine their research contexts, paying attention to existing relationships obscured by Western frameworks for knowledge. As LeAnne Howe points out, Indigenous scholarship also "consciously use[s] *story, history* and *theory* as interchangeable words because the difference in their usage is artificially constructed" (42). Lee Maracle similarly claims "there is story in every line of theory" (7). In respect for and response to Maracle's call to rhetorically reintegrate things falsely separated, this book is a mix of history, theory, and story.

While this work is informed and benefits from decolonial theory, I do not want to claim that it is necessarily a decolonial project. I understand that decoloniality is more than disciplinary reform and respect the critique that using the term *decolonial* dilutes its material meaning and distracts from real efforts to repatriate stolen lands (Tuck and Yang). Although I hope an academic book might be a node on the networks that produce such fundamental change, I understand that it cannot produce such change on its own. What I will claim instead is that the insights of decolonial theory can provide a way to pause, reflect, and alter our actions in response to Western frameworks that fail to account for the agency of incarcerated writers and that still assess the value of their work in capitalist terms. My hope is that this book can begin a conversation that includes the insights of Indigenous scholars, and that those insights can begin to allow us to see other options and opportunities for our work as scholar-activist teachers.

### ARTS IN CORRECTIONS IN (A PERSONAL) CONTEXT

I grew up in Northern California during what my friend Marty calls "The Golden Age of Arts in Corrections." At that time, my parents' house was occasionally full of musicians, poets, sculptors, actors, and makers of paper crafts, flutes, guitars, and beaded jewelry. The artists who came with wine, bread, and ripe tomatoes were employees of the Department of Corrections—artist facilitators hired to oversee AIC programs at each of California's thirty-three prisons. In his twenty-five years with AIC, my dad, Jim Carlson,[2] served as an artist facilitator at San Quentin, an administrator overseeing the implementation of arts programs in all state prisons, and an artist facilitator again at New Folsom, where he worked until 2014.

Carlson was hired at San Quentin in 1984, seven years after AIC first began, funded by a curious patchwork of local and national agencies.[3] In 1981 the California legislature appropriated $400,000

Photo by Peter Merts.

to augment the Department of Corrections budget, and Arts in Corrections officially became a unit within the Department of Corrections under the umbrella of Community Resource Development (Arts-in-Corrections). Over the next thirty years, a series of contractors, most notably the William James Association and ArtsReach (UCLA Extension), oversaw the hiring, training, and managing of the contract teaching artists who were dispatched to each institution for residencies of varying length.

The AIC program is an example of the type of collaborative sponsorships that cropped up around the country in the 1970s and 1980s.[4] It was an official unit within the California Department of Corrections and Rehabilitation (CDCR) with a permanent budget line in the California state budget. By the 1990s, state funds were being used to employ artist facilitators at prisons across the state. Artist facilitators, who were also professional artists, often taught classes in their area of expertise, functioned as intermediaries between the institution and the community, oversaw the day-to-day work of additional contract teaching artists, and showed up at our house once a year to report on their work and share stories.

Through this collaborative sponsorship model, incarcerated men and women were able to access professional instruction in "painting, drawing, sculpture, murals, photography, poetry, creative writing, theater, and music" (Arts-in-Corrections). By the 1990s, AIC had become the "largest institutionally-based arts program in the United States" (Arts-in-Corrections). In 2003, AIC lost its funding and artist facilitators were absorbed into the Department of Corrections' Education Department. This shift required the AIC program to give up its autonomy and classroom-based instructional model for a more rigid and less effective bureaucratic and pedagogical structure. Artist facilitators were tasked with distributing a stripped-down, in-cell arts curriculum inconsistent with AIC's relational model of classroom-based instruction.

Nonetheless, the move kept the program alive (at least technically) for an additional seven years. At New Folsom, Carlson received strong administrative support from the Education department that allowed him to keep the art room open. A mix of volunteers and incarcerated artists taught classes, and the inmate clerking posts that provided some administrative support for the program were also retained. These posts allowed incarcerated teachers to be paid prison wages to teach and to organize the group offerings. These incarcerated artists capably stood in the gap left when the professional teachers from the community lost their posts, continuing to provide quality fine arts instruction.

Along with others, Carlson helped cobble together administrative and financial support from the Inmate Welfare Fund, the Sacramento Poetry Center, and a local church. The church was especially helpful, providing funds to pay the volunteer teachers, purchase arts materials, and professionally record and produce music written, arranged, and performed by incarcerated musicians. Then, in January 2010, under the auspices of a well-publicized state budget crisis, the CDCR eliminated the reassigned remains of the AIC program. Carlson reinvented himself once again as a recreational therapist at New Folsom and kept the program going by shifting the locus of support to mental health, connecting AIC to federally mandated program offerings. In sum, he worked with others to patiently tie, re-tie, and add new relational threads in an effort to keep the program alive.

When I began as a volunteer teacher at New Folsom in 2009, I walked into what appeared to be the final rending of incarcerated artists from decades of sanctioned opportunities to use both state and community sponsorship to create materials of their choosing in a dynamic, relational space. The AIC room at New Folsom that I entered in 2009 was, in every way, the culmination of seventeen years of financial investment in arts materials and instruction coupled with nearly two decades of goodwill politics between the incarcerated artists, Carlson, and the prison administration. It was a bureaucratic anomaly and a beleaguered bastion for the arts with important political connections at every level. These connections had afforded the AIC a slow death, but it seems sure that the long and creative struggle to keep the program going was coming to an end.

It was a raw moment. Those associated with the program seemed to be quietly and not so quietly grieving a deep loss. The AIC program had been able to enact tacit yet significant disruptions to business as usual at the prison—respectful guards, classes taught by incarcerated artists, uncensored cross-racial dialogues, public performances on the yard—but the financial crisis had rendered these gains disposable. And on a personal level, my dad received his pink slip when he was turning sixty and waiting on some potentially scary medical reports. It was through the portal of these overlapping programmatic and personal crises that I entered the AIC classroom as a teacher and a daughter.

This text draws on my own tangled, complicated relationship to the AIC program. Though the stories I tell here are personal, I don't think this fact negates their scholarly value. I have chosen not to pretend an academic detachment that Eber Hampton suggests is not possible anyway for scholars anywhere. Like Lee Maracle, I consider the separation of theory and story—words that "prove" from words that "show"—to be a futile exercise. I have interwoven my own stories throughout this book with the voices of scholars—some dead, some still around; some famous, others less so. I circle back throughout the text to a few key stories (the performance of *Waiting for Godot* and the filming of *At Night I Fly* [Wenzer] in particular) where they inform the greater discussion. Furthermore, because I imagine that all the actors in my story have something to say, I have tried to leave space even for the walls to talk.

The stories both heard and witnessed at New Folsom—of classroom spaces where rival gang members share their poems and public audiences visit the prison for artistic performances—are hard-won in prison, so I began to ask how AIC had survived at New Folsom as long as it had beyond the program's official demise. What I found, and what I discuss in this book, is that the success of AIC at New Folsom can be attributed in large part to a model that values and evaluates opportunities over individual behavioral outcomes. Furthermore, without describing their work in these terms, Carlson and his colleagues had built a program based on a relational methodology.

After one year as a volunteer AIC teacher, I started a PhD program to examine, through academic theory, what was happening in and to AIC. Drawing on my experiences at New Folsom, I attempted to inform my scholarly work with the dialectic concepts of opportunity and relationality, only to find that the structures of academic inquiry work against both notions in tangible ways.[5] As I will discuss later, the IRB process demanded revisions that relabeled Spoon and Marty my subjects instead of my teaching colleagues. Most of the scholarship I was reading was written by men who were dead, white, and French. My classmates found that my articulations of the work at New Folsom lacked revolutionary verve. The psychic disequilibrium, to use Adrienne Rich's term, of those early grad school days was unsettling.

At some point I shared the jumble of my thoughts with Kristin Arola. In response, she suggested I read *Research Is Ceremony* by Shawn Wilson, which became a point of entry for me into the conversation about Indigenous methodologies and decolonial work. I understood then, as I understand now, that my position as a white woman functioning at the intersection of two hulking institutions built on and sustained by systemic injustice complicates my relationship to this important body of work. And I take seriously the admonition laid out by Arola and Arola in their essay on assemblage:

> Even if our objective is to create in such a way as to open up new worlds of possibility in response to a confrontation with problems that we presently lack the resources to resolve, we still must be cautious that our employment of and engagement with the world do not unconsciously repeat and reinforce the world from which we are attempting to find lines of flight. This requires attention, attentiveness not just to individual concepts, ideas, or images, but to the neighborhoods they inhabit and their genesis. (219)

Keeping all of this in mind, I've approached my analysis of prison writing through the lens of decoloniality and relationality. While I could turn to actor-network theory, or feminist new materialisms, or other Western theories to do this work, I turn to Indigenous theory and decoloniality because more than any other theory I have encountered, it calls me, as a white woman, to also think through my intentions, to disrupt my colonial constructs, and to rethink what it means to engage in literacy projects. As Zoe Todd has pointed out, within the academy there is a *"continued, collective* reticence to address its own racist and colonist roots, and the debt to Indigenous thinkers in a meaningful and structural way" (10). Such theory demands I account for my own position throughout this text as one who has benefited from the larger colonial structures that have denied those same benefits to others. It also places me in the complex position of invoking the insights of scholars who have been historically oppressed by these structures. And yet to deny such complexities is to continue this oppression. So while I understand I may face critique for using Indigenous theories as a white woman focusing on prisons, I believe ignoring any theories that can help us disrupt identities and structures premised on coloniality is a way of enabling further violence.

Furthermore, I do not presume that my suggestions informed by Indigenous theory "can solve the problem of mass incarceration." As Daniel Karpowitz has pointed out, "this deadly phenomenon . . . can only be addressed by putting fewer people in prison and for less time; by making our economy less punitive; and by eliminating the stark racial disparities that mar all aspects of American inequality and especially criminal justice" (25). I do not pretend that the classroom spaces I am co-creating at New Folsom are putting fewer people in prison or making our economy less punitive. But I can work in earnest to articulate and join the type of local delinking efforts that Ellen Cushman has suggested are "sow[ing] the seeds of pluriversal realities within composition studies, realities that could well change both the disciplinary and pedagogical tenets and contents of the field." I take seriously Cushman's call for the development of "more decolonial possibilities through research and teaching that are dedicated to leveling the social, epistemic, semiotic, and linguistic hierarchies that (de)humanize us all" ("Translingual" 235). I also know that as a non-Indigenous person working in a prison where some participants are Indigenous, I cannot (and would not) claim that what I am articulating reflects tribal knowledge, which varies and is specific to place and community. But scholars such as Wilson, Cordova, and Deloria have constructed key frameworks that share Indigenous methods/philosophies/ideologies such as respect, responsibility, reciprocity, and relationality, and I hope to show the value such insights might offer those working in prison classrooms with the acknowledgment that this version, like any flattening of Indigenous theory, is always incomplete. Indigenous theory, and the questions it asks about what is real and how we know it to be such, pushes scholars outside of the narrow, individuated paradigm of Western thought and thus offers an ethically grounded place from which to imagine what the options for decolonial work might look like. This particular body of scholarly work also legitimates Audre Lorde's question about whether the master's house can be dismantled with the master's tools. If modernity's toolbox is full of tools that help scholars denigrate and dehumanize through processes that autonomize, individuate, and economically commodify, then different tools are sorely needed.

### ARTS IN CORRECTIONS IN (AN ECONOMIC) CONTEXT

As both Richard Miller and Ian Hunter have noted, educational programs have never been rational enterprises, but rather "product[s] of a series of complex, contradictory, compromised, and contingent solutions whose permanence is never assured" (Miller 8). To believe otherwise is to be drawn more deeply "into the teacher's fallacy" (Hunter 34). Yet the siren song of logic, and particularly of economic logics, is still used to justify the effectiveness of these programs. This is particularly true in prison, where scholar-teachers feel compelled to use economic logics to prove that their programs are worthy—and, in doing so, promote the very perspectives that helped the prison grow in the first place.

Ellen Cushman has pointed out that economic logics are a central part of the "colonial matrices of power . . . built on intersecting, mutually sustaining nodes of everyday logics of practice that form disciplines and universities" ("Translingual" 237). Likewise, Wendy

Brown observes that a governing neoliberal logic or "order of normative reason" exists that extends "a specific formulation of economic value, practices, and metrics to every dimension of human life" (30). This logic shows up on university campuses in the conversations regarding "return on investment" (ROI), a metric used by families shopping for high-value college experiences. In prison education, ROI is often understood primarily through recidivism statistics. This is, of course, a valuable measurement, but measuring a reduction in recidivism alone cannot tell whole stories about how both individuals and groups break their ties to prison.

Consider Charles, a key AIC participant at New Folsom who is currently serving a life without parole sentence. In his case, recidivism is a useless measure for evaluating success. At the same time, Charles's story is one of a family defying the statistics about intergenerational incarceration and breaking its ties to prison: his kids have all made it to college. And although Charles's AIC experience isn't the only reason for his children's success, there are a host of connections between the opportunities Charles made for himself through AIC as a student and teacher and his identity as a citizen and parent. For example, at one point, some of the musicians in the AIC program were able to write and record music that was then professionally mixed. Charles contributed as a vocalist to the project and was able to share those recordings with his kids. He also features prominently in *At Night I Fly*, the 2011 film about AIC at New Folsom (Wenzer).

Beyond the contributions he has made to his family and a few notable artistic products, Charles also played a key role in sustaining AIC within the institution. He was a program manager, well positioned and adept at protecting the room from the fallout of racial and gang politics; Carlson largely credits him for making sure that AIC classes at New Folsom were free of violence and other infractions. In Charles's story we see the same relational complexities between classroom, visiting room, and community that are present in Bryson's story. We also see the complications inherent in the idea of individual narratives of transformation, which continue to be overpraised and overcirculated.

The effects of the AIC program on both Bryson and Charles might be better represented by circles or webs than by straight teleological lines. Although endgame constructions can sometimes be productive, they are too often accompanied by a focus on expediency (Bury). As Steven Katz points out, expediency as a core value of any project can be dangerous. In the context of prison writing programs, speed and efficiency can be particularly commodifying by working together to constrain who and what scholar-teachers are willing to study.

Unfortunately, the challenge of locating appropriate avenues for collecting empirical evidence leaves prison arts programs vulnerable to study designs that are unproductively narrow, obscure, and patronizing. Halperin and colleagues conducted the largest empirical study to date of prison arts programs, which has been widely cited by AIC advocates in their conversations with state legislators and other financial stakeholders. The study is a prime example of how economic and colonial logics come tightly paired and work against the liberatory aims of education. To find a measurable claim, Halperin et al. studied whether arts programs "may motivate those with long sentences to pursue educational degrees" (6). At face value, the study seems innocuous enough, yet the justification that Halperin et al. provide for it highlights a troubling attention to efficacy. They suggest that a "skeptical researcher, prison administrator, or politician could claim that most evidence for the efficacy of prison arts programs is weak because there is no way to determine that it is the specific enrichment program that actually creates positive change in the participants" (8). Here the need for efficacy is coupled with the need for an individual narrative of transformation, where the incarcerated participant becomes a passive recipient of economically advantageous behavioral change.

Halperin and colleagues' economic justification for the study exemplifies how the "market value of knowledge—its income-enhancing prospects for individuals and industry alike—is now understood as both its driving purpose and leading line of defense" for educational projects (W. Brown 187). The study authors explain that previous studies have not been able to defend the possibility that "a special kind of inmate—one predisposed to succeed in prison and post-release—elects to participate in these kinds of voluntary programs" (8). In an effort to find an empirically defensible argument, Halperin et al. narrow the value of non-credit-bearing work to its ability to encourage credit-bearing work, thereby devaluing—and maybe even openly discouraging—a study of how this "special kind of inmate" might "succeed in prison and post-release." Furthermore, the "special kind of inmate" language is demeaning, setting up an unnecessary (and undefined) binary between *regular* and *special* that more deeply abstracts and dehumanizes the nuanced experiences of incarcerated people. In sum, the type of methodology used by Halperin et al.—their whittling down of complex human stories in search of an elusive X factor—cannot account for the value of a program like AIC for either Charles or Bryson.

Halperin et al. are not alone in employing an economic logic that subsumes non-credit-bearing educational work in service to postsecondary education (Brewster, *An Evaluation,* "California"). At the 2014 National Arts in Corrections Conference, I pointed out the potential for unintended negative outcomes with this line of logic and was met with resistance by scholar-teachers who suggested that something is better than nothing and that using empirical, economic vocabulary would help increase the likelihood of receiving Pell Grant funding. Thus, the conversation was redirected back to a near-sighted focus on how to capture and capitalize on scarce resources.

The "hurry and do something while you can" argument ubiquitous since the reinstatement of Pell Grants for incarcerated students is at odds with the advice of William Cleveland in *Teaching the Arts behind Bars,* where he asks practitioners to "steel [themselves] to thinking 'small, slow, less'" (R. Williams 34). But small, slow, and less is a difficult move in the face of injustice, sorrow, and horror. Scholar-teachers in prison are understandably inclined to speed of all kinds—speed away from the prison to shake off what we witness there, and speed toward anything and everything that might mediate or end the suffering that defines prison. But working with speed implies trajectory, and rhetorics of trajectory are closely related to rhetorics of transformation. Usually, when we are in a hurry, we are in a hurry to see things change. This is not to say that things should *not* change, but rather that words like *change, transformation,* and *speed* have a sordid history in the context of colonial history.

A greater critical awareness of the limits and dangers of economic thinking has shown up in prison scholarship since the reinstatement of Pell Grants for prisoners. Rob Scott points out that "recidivism is amongst the only outcomes to fit positivism's narrow horizon of testable and measurable results" ("Using" 411). Erin Castro and Michael Brawn similarly suggest that "postsecondary education in prison pivots on a narrow and faulty logic of reduced recidivism" (101). In asking prison scholar-teachers to move beyond "a trivially simple quantitative analysis," Scott suggests that "prison educators must be careful not to become so focused on data and outcomes that our research loses its critical potential" (411). Maybe most pointedly, Marie Gottschalk suggests "the narrow emphasis on evidence-based research related to recidivism fosters the impression that the birth of the carceral state was the result of bad or nonexistent research rather than bad politics or bad policy" (17). Even with strong voices pushing back and making a bit of space, those critical of economic logics find themselves at odds with funding requirements for demonstrations of individual transformation (namely reduced recidivism) and accelerated, economically efficient timeframes for generating such evidence.

Telling the full, complex stories of incarcerated people involves recognizing not only the whole person in the classroom, but also the overlapping systems of injustice and oppression of which mass incarceration in the United States is but a part. The story of how mass incarceration fits into the broader narrative of injustice in the United States is finding widespread public attention, particularly as told by such figures as Michelle Alexander and Ava DuVernay. Both of these storytellers have persuasively shown mass incarceration in the United States to be a systemic problem.

Of course, all important social issues are deeply complicated and require nuanced, multi-faceted responses. In this case, slowing or stemming the rate at which people return to prison should indeed be part of a much broader calculus for reducing the imprint of prisons on society, but focusing on the individual at the exclusion of other factors does little more than "repeat and reinforce the world from which [prison scholars and activists] are attempting to find lines of flight" (Arola and Arola). Because teachers of writing have been part of the US prison landscape since its beginning, coming to terms with their complicity in the structures that govern incarceration policy and practice is paramount.

Scholar-teachers looking for decolonial options may find a way forward in Ellen Cushman's observation that "delinking efforts have sown the seeds of pluriversal realities within composition studies, realities that could well change both the disciplinary and pedagogical tenets and contents of the field." Although Cushman is referring here to translingual approaches to composition, a robust effort to delink prison pedagogy from an economically expedient and individualistic frame can add to the body of decolonial research "dedicated to leveling the social, epistemic, semiotic, and linguistic hierarchies that (de)humanize us all" ("Translingual" 235).

Although, as Cushman has suggested, decolonial projects cannot merely pivot the center, there have been important moves in the field to develop a posture of respect with writers and partners outside the university, and these moves have helped make space for a more expansive attention to issues of respect and reciprocity. Part of that work has been a closer attention to listening. But the conversation around listening needs to be expanded even further. A practice of rhetorical listening as described by scholars like Krista Ratcliffe and Stephanie Kerschbaum might help allay the historical imbalance between speaking and listening for individuals but cannot completely mediate the effects of colonial structures that conscribe the relationship between scholar-practitioners and the greater community.

Nonetheless, listening to voices other than the ones we are used to hearing and dispensing with the obsession of listening for concrete answers (Gilyard; hooks) can move scholars closer to a sensibility that replaces the notion of *answer* with something closer to Walter Mignolo's decolonial *options*. But even this shift cannot ensure that the relationship between the scholar-teacher and the community is decolonial. A truly decolonial project, after all, requires a reordering of this relationship. The Indigenous understanding that relationships "do not merely shape reality, [but rather] are reality" provides a foundation for imagining what such a reordered relationship might look like (S. Wilson 7). But a firm foundation is only the beginning. Recognizing the relational shape of reality does not magically create the relational alliances necessary for building respectful and reciprocal program models that, one hopes, chip away at systemic injustice.

## THE AGENCY (AND RELATIONALITY) OF A SPLIT SANDWICH

The US prison grows with terrifying speed. The horrors of the place and its well-documented record of destroying communities, ravaging families, and dehumanizing US citizens shame its alleged reformatory intention. Much has been said about the prison as a political economic machine[6] and about its connections to systemic racism.[7] The realities of the US prison in the twenty-first century have led to arguments for its dismantling (A. Davis, *Are Prisons*). Since a significant and compelling body of scholarship already exists on the *what* and *why* of prison, such arguments will not be reiterated here. However, I do want to say a word about the notion of resistance and position myself as someone who supports acts of resistance and disruption with the same commitment and energy as I do all the articulated goals of the writers who come to class.

Early on in my experience talking about prison with my colleagues in the academy, I found myself silenced when I suggested that not all the incarcerated men I had met wanted to participate in the revolution that my colleagues on campus were insisting was a key part of any prison abolition movement. I took some of the conversation from campus back to the prison classroom. The dialogue that ensued was as mixed as I expected. Some participants advocated violence as a means to revolution. Others did not. One man got really agitated. He stood, started waving his arms, and stepped back from the table, saying, "This isn't fuckin' Attica. I am not interested in that shit." His comment continues to shape my interest in the conversation about authorial purposes and the deep need to show respect for incarcerated writers even and perhaps especially when they do not share my own philosophical orientation.

The need for real and immediate change is obvious and palpable in prison, but what counts as change, and whose interests it serves, is much less clear. It is in the murky waters between the shores of radical prison abolition and a racialized judicial system that all sponsors of prison writing function. I understand that I am complicit in this structure. But I also understand that every single conversation I have had in the prison—in the classroom, in the sally port, in the cellblock—has ultimately ended with me walking out the front gate and back to my life outside the walls. I take seriously the physical, emotional, spiritual, and psychological danger that hovers ever and always in and around the lives of incarcerated men and women, and I work to remember that they must live—some for the rest of their lives—in a place that I only visit.

Jason Haslam articulates the complicated nature of prison writing when he suggests that studying it "inextricably tangles the material and cultural, the contemporary and the historical, the activist and the analyst, the personal and the public." He points out that the whole endeavor hinges on a hopeful paradox: that the study of prison writing bring about "its own obsolescence" (479). In identifying this paradox, Haslam echoes Miles Horton's admonition that we keep "our eyes on the ought to be" (Branch). At its most hopeful and most agentive, prison writing *does* lead to its own obsolescence when incarcerated writers are able to leave the prison system. However, most of the incarcerated writers who speak in this text are serving life without parole sentences, which means that they will only ever leave prison in body bags, either by violence, illness, or old age. So even as I share Haslam's hope, I see that the conversation about agency must also attend to something other than obvious acts of transformation or liberation.

As I have observed it at New Folsom, agency rarely takes the form of emancipation or tells grand narratives of victory. More often it's a matter of getting a thirty-foot rope into San Quentin for performances of *Waiting for Godot* or taking a guitar back to the cellblock. It looks like Northern and Southern Mexican gang members smuggling poems to each other through an intermediary, since gang code demands that all face-to-face encounters occur with makeshift weapons in hand. Sometimes it looks like the penning of a political essay for an independent Bay-area newspaper. Most days, though, it looks like fifteen men in blue shirts sitting around a table writing as fast as they can.

Individual agency in prison might even look as ordinary as having the choice to split a sandwich. In one of the most powerful scenes from *At Night I Fly* (Wenzer), a heated conversation breaks out between AIC participants discussing cross-racial friendship. The conversation begins after Jack, who is white, admits that although the classroom camaraderie and mutual respect is important to him, he is unwilling to acknowledge his cross-racial friendships on the yard, with its rigid and often bloody racialized codes. That scene was likely filmed in 2003.

I met Jack in an intensive journaling class seven years later in 2010. In my class, he wrote about an event in which inmates ate with visiting community members. Real food was served—sandwiches with lunch meat, mayo, fresh lettuce, and tomato. Jack wrote about reaching for the last sandwich left only to have a black inmate ask him to split it. He draws the reader into his very real and serious dilemma, pondering the consequences of this one racialized act. In the end, he split the sandwich. When Jack finished reading the piece to the class, another writer in the group, Eugene, admitted that he was the man with whom Jack had shared the sandwich. Eugene told Jack how important that moment was for him and marked it as significant in his own process of building cross-racial trust.

The two men stood to hug. As I watched, I did not understand that Jack had been weighing the choice to publicly out himself as a wavering white supremacist for the better part of a decade. When I realized how long it took Jack to make the choice to share the sandwich and then eventually write about it, I knew we needed theories and methodologies for the classroom that could make sense of and support protracted relational processes. I don't know that Jack was transformed in a permanent sense after splitting the sandwich; he was transferred shortly after the incident. But I do know that during his ten years at New Folsom, Jack grappled in very real ways with issues of relationality and relational accountability, and that he used his limited agency to build relationships of consequence.

Taking up a critique of the structures and epistemological underpinnings of a discipline might seem like a fool's errand akin to shouting at a wall or scooping water from the sea. Yet I do not imagine that bureaucracies—of imprisonment or education—are too monolithic or too vast to be moved by increments. This text presumes that congruence between what we desire and what we do is indeed possible; that a situated, albeit contingent, agency is possible for both incarcerated writers and literacy sponsors within the academy. Such agency is a living thing that must be tended, and doing so within a cruel and illogical bureaucratic apparatus is an active, relational business.

## WHERE WE GO FROM HERE

The three remaining academic chapters of this book discuss the importance of paying attention to relationality in the prison writing classroom, how to put such attention into practice, and relevant examples from New Folsom. In Chapter 2, I explore the work of global decolonial scholars such as Sabelo J. Ndlovu-Gatsheni and Siphamandla Zondi and Ngūgī wa Thiong'o who speak to the need to "re-member" the people, places, and processes torn apart by colonization, then offer an abbreviated review of the literature on prison writing vis-à-vis relationality and finally a retelling of AIC's relational origin story. In Chapter 3, I draw on the work of Shawn Wilson to convey the importance of relational accountability within the AIC program at New Folsom and offer a framework for building ethical and relational methodologies into prison-based programs based on the work of Margaret Kovach. Finally, in Chapter 4, I provide specific examples of relationality as manifested in the history of the AIC and discuss the impact of this theory on two current AIC projects.

Before, between, and after the academic chapters, I have placed narrative selections from current and former AIC participants as well as some of my own creative writing about teaching in prison. These selections are intended to invite the reader more deeply into the life of AIC at New Folsom. Each of these pieces shows the effects of relationality on prison-scholars and upends the misconception that these writers and their teachers exist somehow apart from the web of relations beyond the prison walls.

# WRITERS AND TEACHERS, PART 2

**Why I Write**

There is something preventing me from getting to sleep. Nothing out of the ordinary, but I know I have to reconcile with something. I tried hard to come up with a closing line to a story and felt like a failure for two years. But I continued to write around my failure so atrophy wouldn't settle in, along with my ignorance.

I write to see for myself. I write to catch my breath. I write to make sure I saw it. I write to remember. I write to forget. I write because blank pages taunt me. I write because books haunt me. I write because I hear things when no one is around. I write because I don't have tattoos or business cards. I write because when I bleed it doesn't always hurt. I write to my enemies. I write because school's out. I write to burn incense. I write in the dark sometimes to see if it stays the same in the light. I write unintentionally. I write the clown's makeup off his face. I write because it's expected. I write because it's neglected. I write to see if words still work. I write the windows. I write to give my issues issues of their own. I write because it's believable. I write to fight outside my weight class. I write the sand out of the sandbox. I write so when they point at me I can point at something too. I write because my dad couldn't. I write because my mom could. I write because my sister still does. I write because I'm right handed. I write to be remembered. I write to be responsible. I write to get a good grade. I write the colors. I write in *extra* long hand. I write because a psych costs too much. I write because there is no other way. I write because tears aren't enough. I write in the jokes. I write to feed my homeless thoughts. I write because I might be homeless. I write myself dry. I write because I am inconsistent and spontaneous. I write because there's more people than places. I write because I know my place. I write because I look better written. I don't write as much as I should. I write myself to sleep. I write for the thrill of belonging. I write in my bible. I write pain's name over and over. I write to prisoners. I write around funeral processions. I write because I'm emotionally constipated. I write to keep from eating. I write to keep from drowning. I write because I was wrong. I write the wrongs. I write because my prom sucked. I write to get there. I write because there's no such thing as a bad T-ball game. I write because I have a time limit. I write to stop time.

And when time stops, I read. I read books like menus, ordering one of each.

—Harry B. Grant Jr.

**The Circle**

Okay, it's your turn, Wayne.
Draw a circle, said the teacher.

I'm five years old
and my penis is still healing
from the vicious kick the white kid
gave me with those pointy boots I kept staring at.

Sucks to have never seen
cowboy boots and your first introduction
is ever
memorialized.

I waddle to the front of the class
all the while escorted with snickers and
comments under breath
that I can't hear but fully understand
when I catch words from behind me
            kicked in the penis
            kept staring at his boots

The teacher hands me a piece of chalk
and I draw a circle
thinking of riding on my grandpa's shoulders
as he waded easily over the waist high snow.

I put the chalk down and
a wave of Ooohs and Aaahs
pleasant and warm brush over me.

That's the best circle I've ever seen, Wayne.

It felt great. I did something pleasing.
It made me feel good.

When I sat down I couldn't help thinking,
What's the big deal? It's a circle.

I thought maybe
if I would have drawn a circle earlier I
wouldn't have gotten kicked in the dick
for staring at someone's boots.

—Wayne Vaka

**Ceremony**

Ten minutes into class I am interrupted. A class Regular—cat-like, prone to pacing—pushes his chair back, lets his pencil fall, roll away. "I'm trippin' right now and I can't concentrate because somebody died this morning. I'm really trippin' on that." Heads are raised all around the table; I watch souls swimming through the flat affect of psychotropic drugs and fluorescent lighting, swimming upstream towards a raw patch of connection. More chairs push back.

"We never get news when our people die."

"There is no way to grieve here."

"From my cell I can see the graveyard at Old Folsom. It's pretty fuckin' sad. You should go there. That's where they bury the bodies no one comes to get."

"Shit, no one is coming for me."

The bald man across from me folds his arms across his chest. He is probably thirty-five. I don't know anything about him. He says that the worst of prison is not the loss of physical freedom. He speaks quietly from his experience. "We don't get to feel feelings and nobody here stops to honor the dead. Death is everywhere here, but we walk around it, act like we don't see."

The freshness of the departed and each man's confession of loss thickens the musty room with all the dead suddenly invited, rushing in from their wailing and roaming, looking for an eye, a tear, a word of burial. When the air can accommodate no more words, we get out paper. Some write quickly into safer pasture. But four pencils are obedient to the particular visions of death resting heavy between their shoulders. When it is time to read, we let the writers hosting ghosts go last. We blanket the ghosts in warm silence then speak the dead man's prison nickname since no one knows the name given to him by his parents.

The man who had made the day's initial invitation asks to pray. His words soften as they are absorbed around the room, soaking into shirts and skin. He finds his voice, begins to breathe. "Jesus, we pray for our dead Brother and ask you to take his soul. Please look after him and take him home." I am working to be present, to honor the moment, but my mind splinters as it tries to reconcile the particular paradox of this witness. I think of the public story of this man's violent crime—Vesuvius and blistering ash—an eruption of mental illness and drug use.

I ask the walls, *Can two things be true at the same time?*

I will learn later that unclaimed bodies are not at the Old Folsom Cemetery. I will learn this from a mortician who held the state contract for two years but lost the bid to a guy who could handle the State's bodies for ten dollars less per head. He explains the process anyway: the gurney is checked at each door to make sure only the dead are leaving; the State pays for a cremation; emergency contacts are notified; the ashes of life are handed back in awkward, embarrassed silence. When emergency contacts don't call back, when three months pass, the ashes are added to a potter's field, mixed into the clay that does not grow things, lacks humus.

He does not miss the contract; turns out it was not worth the hassle. Most inmates die somewhere else. Most inmates spend their Folsom years in the acceptable health of midlife.

—Anna Plemons

# 2

## The Process of Re-Membering: The Case for Relationality as Decolonial Practice

> [For] any kind of restorative work to succeed, there must be constant contact and exchange with the public, people of all ages, colors, and cultures. There must be continuous dialog and programs that put mirrors up to everyone's faces, not just the prisoners.
>
> — Judith Tannenbaum and Spoon Jackson,
> *By Heart: Poetry, Prison, and Two Lives*

THE FIRST STORY I HEARD THAT HELPED me understand the importance of relationality in the prison classroom is a story Carlson tells about teaching juggling at San Quentin in the 1980s. He says that not long after he started teaching the juggling class, an attendee mentioned that two new things had happened for him: he had heard real laughter on the yard for the first time, and he had crumpled paper in the visiting room and used it to teach his young sons how to juggle during a weekend visit. He told Carlson it was the first time he had been able to teach his sons anything since his incarceration.

As this story shows, many incarcerated students are already looking for opportunities to reconnect to their place in the world outside prison. Relationality is part of the prison classroom whether or not we realize or care to acknowledge it. This story also points to the need for a broader calculus of what should count and be counted as valuable in prison education. Building on the story of the juggling father, this chapter furthers the conversation about why a close attention to the principles of relationality is a timely project for the field of composition as we continue to grapple with how to incorporate the insights of decolonial theory and practices into our work. Scholarship on relationality makes some space for pedagogies that allow scholar-teachers to purposefully join with incarcerated people in the hard work of reconnecting what incarceration so violently separates. And the list of things that incarceration violently separates is long so there are many points of entry for work that aims to reconnect what has been rent apart. Of course, small, local acts of relational reconnection will not, on their own, crumble the concrete. But listening and responding to the relational threads of a classroom can afford teachers in the prison opportunities to support incarcerated students as they work to position themselves as integral parts of families and communities beyond the walls.

### THE DECOLONIAL WORK OF RE-MEMBERING

As established in Chapter 1, the US prison system is a modern crisis situated within global histories of colonialization. Scholar-teachers must recognize this colonial context if they are to engage with incarcerated students, and those in higher education must be no less mindful of the colonial contexts of their colleges and universities. Scholar-teachers in the prison thus find themselves caught within overlapping colonial contexts and pressed into existing tracks that might tease the boundary lines but can never quite escape the ideological perimeter of coloniality.

Global decolonial scholarship provides some key terms that help name both the macro and micro processes that continue to animate the practice of coloniality. In particular, the idea of *dismemberment* describes a relational reality in which parts of a whole are unnaturally separated. Borrowing a term from Ngũgĩ wa Thiong'o, Ndlovu-Gatsheni and Zondi write that university student movements in South Africa are demanding a "re-membering" that purposefully works against colonial processes. These students' grievances are echoed among incarcerated people in the United States who have themselves been "dismembered" from society at large. In the United States, the humanity of incarcerated people has regularly been questioned. The language of "super-predators" first adopted by John Dilulio in 1995 and popularized by Hillary Clinton provides just one example (Drum). Michelle Alexander and others have already aptly drawn the connections between enslavement and incarceration, and Ruth Wilson Gilmore has carefully described the political processes by which the prison industrial complex has grown.

Whereas Ndlovu-Gatsheni and Zondi claim that the reproduction of coloniality in Africa has been mainly rolled out by the "African elites who inherited the colonial state," in the case of the US prison there has been a tragically seamless handoff from public educators to judiciary and prison administrators to prison educators, as outlined by Erica Meiners in her work on the school-to-prison pipeline ("Ending"). Meiners highlights the role teachers and school administrators play in tracking young students away from educational opportunities and ultimately toward incarceration, thus dismembering them from opportunities for educational attainment. In this context, scholar-teachers arriving at the prison doors bearing pencils and transformational rhetorics seem less like shining beacons of liberation than cogs in the larger colonial system.

Although scholars often use the word *erasure* to describe the social effect on incarcerated people, a theory of relationality challenges the accuracy of the term. It is true, of course, that incarcerated people are systematically made physically invisible by their incarceration, but invisibility and erasure are not synonymous: where the one suggests a mere obscuring from view, the other suggests a total disappearance from society. A rhetoric of erasure encourages scholar-teachers in US prisons to see incarcerated people as autonomous and free of any relational contexts. Most scholar-teachers have no idea how their incarcerated students might dress outside of prison, let alone anything about their roots, their work, or their family lives. All of this helps explain the ubiquity of individualized narratives of transformation. Precisely because incarceration obscures, scholar-teachers need to acknowledge their students' larger web of relations and support them as they seek to be re-membered, through their writing, as personal and cultural assets in communities outside the prison.

A prison pedagogy of re-membering, then, works to disrupt the commodification of incarcerated people, both in the economic and political processes that come at their expense as well as the hyper-focus on individual progress (rehabilitation and reduced recidivism) that still justifies the existence of prison education programs. Though an attention to relationality cannot singularly solve either of those daunting systemic problems, it can offer a solid pedagogical foundation on which to build specific practices and processes. Specifically, prison research and pedagogy can help re-member incarcerated students in at least three key ways. Prison scholar-teachers can challenge popular language about incarcerated people as erased from the communities that are important to them. They can also challenge individual narratives of transformation that abstract incarcerated students' connections to those communities. Last, they can challenge a deficit ideology of incarcerated people as lacking the motivations, interests, and tools needed for community engagement. Instead, teachers can re-member that incarcerated students are often already important cultural assets in communities that are important to them inside and outside the prison. Taken together, the interrelated processes of challenging narratives of erasure, disrupting narratives of individual transformation, and rejecting deficit ideology begins the process of developing a prison pedagogy of re-membering.

The challenge of moving beyond (or around) the hyper-focus on the transformation of the individual is understandable given that the genesis of the modern prison was formed around notions of penitence and reformation. And where penitence was the ends, literacy education was the means (Kahan). Between the penitentiary of the Pennsylvanian Quakers and the machine that is the US prison at present much has changed. But what has not changed is the way that literacy work is fused at the root with ideologies and rhetorics of transformation (Rolston). In the context of the prison classroom, this overly simplistic, causal, and economic relationship between education and material value still often forms the basic argument for literacy sponsorship inside. Like other literacy work, prison writing programs cannot seem to shake the practice of trafficking in transformational narratives even when it seems obvious enough that literacy does not carry, with any notable assurance, an economic value. Of course, this is not to say that literacy does not have value or even to suggest that it lacks material value. Rather, it is to say that the value of literacy for the individuals and communities that acquire and employ it is complicated, contingent, organic, and relational.

The complicated, relational value of literacy is highlighted in Harry B. Grant Jr.'s essay "Why I Write" (pp. 33–34). Beyond the myriad motivations for writing that Grant and others have expressed, length and severity of one's sentence also deeply complicates claims to the economic value of literacy and educational attainment, more broadly. For someone with a life sentence, like Charles from Chapter 1, literacy acquisition does not carry much direct economic promise. Nonetheless, I have heard some really beautiful stories, from Charles and others, about why incarcerated students pursue educational opportunities, and oftentimes those stories describe a value for literacy that is decidedly relational. For example, one AIC student I know recently completed his associate degree and was able to invite his family to the graduation ceremony. He was sixty years old and wanted his grandchildren to see that education is important; he wanted to take on the role of educational patriarch in his family, doing what he could to disrupt the statistical inevitability of intergenerational incarceration.

## THE TROUBLING (DENIAL) OF THE
## YES/AND TRANSFORMATIONAL NARRATIVE

It is important to acknowledge that one reason problematic individual narratives of transformation continue to circulate is that incarcerated writers, working to sort out their own story, continue to write them. Sometimes they write transformational narratives because that is what the teacher is asking of them. But other times they write them because they have invested themselves in the work of making personal change and want to tell that story, want to set things right, want to add their name to the list of those who have made something bright out of a life lived in one of the darkest corners of our society. I understand this drive and I respect the writing it inspires. But I also see the need to critique how folks outside the prison traffic in transformational narratives, and to point out the well-worn disciplinary ruts that draw scholar-teachers back into antiquated ideologies despite our best intentions to go a different way. Transformational narratives, then, need not be anathema but rather crafted and circulated in ways that re-member and respect the nuance and relational complexity in them that is often left largely unexplored, edited out, or ignored.

To demonstrate the thorny nature of transformational narratives I turn to the writings of Spoon Jackson, which have a yes/and quality: he relates his transformational experience of becoming a published poet, *and* he articulates the limits of that transformation and in doing so uncovers some of the relational outcomes of his experiences. In *By Heart* (Tannenbaum and Jackson), Jackson describes the scenes—prison library, prison classroom, prison theatre production—where he "finds his voice" and credits reading and writing with bringing him a sense of purpose and providing him with a creative outlet for reimagining himself.

Jackson's original interest in literacy was urgent, practical, defensive, and solitary: "At first in my prison journey," he writes, "I had just wanted to know what a word meant and how words were constructed into sentences so that high society and political folks like lawyers, doctors, and professors would not be able to say just anything and leave me not understanding" (Tannenbaum and Jackson 13). Over time, though, his utilitarian interest in literacy leads to something else: "I learned a few new words each day and each one brought a geyser erupting inside my mind and soul. The more I read and studied, the clearer life became. I became richer and deeper inside. . . . I had to till the endless gardens in my mind, heart, and soul" (11). Of the library years before he began attending poetry class he writes:

> I went into my cell on Friday afternoon and read and studied until Monday morning. I feasted on knowledge and wisdom. I dived into philosophy, religion, psychology, sociology, ecology, and any "ology" I could get my mind into. I debunked and peeled off layers of false history and propaganda that clogged

my vision, my dreams, and my heart and soul—those misguided histories I had been force-fed like a motherless lamb.

For eight years I had stayed to myself at San Quentin, learning who I was and what I was about. I avoided crowds. Although my heart, mind and soul burned with thoughts, vibes, and feelings, I let none surface and stepped over wounded, dying, or dead bodies as everyone else did. (11)

Jackson's self-education eventually leads him to a poetry class taught by Judith Tannenbaum. In his essay in *Teaching Artist Journal*, Jackson writes that he was initially sure he would not like poetry, dismissing it as the realm of "women, squares, nerds, weirdoes, professors, and highbrows, people caught up in some unreal academic world" ("Speaking"). But he joined Tannenbaum's class anyway, sitting in silence, sunglasses on, just beyond the edge of the circle of students—and something in the class begins to change him. "Now, in Judith's class, I began to embrace words in a new way and to allow words to embrace me," he writes. "Words swarmed inside me like honeybees and took me places—imaginary and true—from the past, present, and future" ("Speaking" 13). Jackson's interest in literacy begins to grow and in some ways to heal some of the wounds left by his early experiences in public school, where he had felt "out of place . . . unheard and unseen" and been repeatedly abused by his teachers (13).

Jackson's reading and writing helped him mentally reposition himself in relationship to both global and national histories as well as his own personal past. In time, his personal relationships at San Quentin began to evolve as well. He accepted a role in *Waiting for Godot*, which allowed his work to circulate in Europe. He met and married a Swedish painter commissioned to paint scenes from the play. He became a published writer and teacher. At one point, many years later after he had been transferred to New Folsom, he was even offered the opportunity to move to a different institution where he could more closely align himself with a university but chose to stay where he was, calling the program he had helped build there "a mecca for the arts." Jackson navigated impossibly narrow constraints without having any strategic control over some of his most basic needs. And yet, as a teaching artist at New Folsom, he got to decide—in one specific moment—whether to move from one institution to another, weighing his relational opportunities as a teaching artist in each place.

Starting in 2010, Jackson's poems, information on his clemency appeal, and links to other material could be found at realnessnetwork.blogspot.com, a website that was built and continues to be maintained by his friends in Sweden. (As of September 2018, the site has had 94,823 views.) Jackson has also had a Twitter account, @SpoonJackson, established in his name that has become the default source for news about his clemency appeal. But Jackson's literacy narrative is not a linear tale with a traditionally happy ending.

Despite his wide public following and strong support for his clemency, Jackson writes of being caught in a double bind. The pursuit of consciousness in prison comes with the painful unrelenting realization that consciousness does not earn anyone physical freedom. "Sometimes I get pissed at the prison system that strives to set people up to fail, even when some prisoners push to help heal and not hinder or destroy," writes Jackson (Tannenbaum and Jackson 191). Despite that reality, Jackson still sees that the work he is doing while incarcerated has value, as he writes in the final lines of his book:

> Forging my path in life is a melancholic mixture of wonder and sadness. I am not happy, nor will I ever be happy, in prison. All I can say is what my character Pozzo said in lines Judith, Jim, Denise, and Jan often quoted during our development of [*Waiting for Godot*]: "That's how it is on this bitch of an earth." I will be released from prison one day, by a beautiful real life or by a beautiful real death. In either case, I have found my niche in life which is something not even death can take away. (192)

Jackson's description of life as a "melancholic mixture of wonder and sadness" and the fact that he may remain incarcerated until his death arrests any impulse to clap or cheer. The closing words of *By Heart* bring the hollow rhetoric of educational salvation into sharp

Photo by Peter Merts.

relief and accentuate the relational dimension of his writing—"a niche in life"—that is out of reach of the prison administration and beyond the clutches of death. There is no happy ending, no grand victory for the transformed individual. And though we might be inclined to shake our fists at the neoliberal state for continuing to hold Jackson, Daniel Karpowitz points out that the obsession with the individual transcends politics. It is not surprising, he writes, that the criminal justice system "focuses on the individual crime, the individual victim, the individual perpetrator—and his or her culpability, containment, and punishment. . . . [T]his individualistic view marks not only the harsh, strong 'right hand' of the state, but also the gentler, welfarist 'left hand'—preoccupied with the transformation of the individual subject" (94).

Those who study and teach composition have largely been unwilling (or more likely unable) to see the ways that the welfarist impulse of the left and the punitive impulse of the right share a philosophical obsession with the individual. Despite the call from Sharon Crowley and others to "focus . . . attention away from individual authors" and toward the community (*Teacher's* 33), many composition scholars, particularly those engaged with off-campus writing communities, still work to justify the value of their programs through individualized narratives of transformation. Linda Flower writes a transformative agenda right into the introduction to her text, calling forth the company of other scholars whose work also aims at transformation through literacy,[1] and examples of the transformative narrative both in the work of incarcerated writers and of program sponsors are ubiquitous.[2] The persistent obsession with evidence of transformation entangles the field of composition in potentially colonial enterprises whereby individual transformations must occur to justify institutional support and where the coin of the realm, articulations of meaning, is required as "payment" for our services.

Often a writing course requires writers to find new meaning in their experiences, which for incarcerated writers can include reckoning with individual criminal acts that are then held up as transformational narratives. For example, Eve Ensler's 2003 documentary *What I Want My Words to Do to You* unabashedly showcases the reflective process of incarcerated women as they "confront the lives they've ruined, the families left behind and their own lives as they might have been." The film ends up mired in the individual confessional statements of the incarcerated writers, and Ensler's own voice in the (re)writing of each woman's criminal act is easy enough to recognize. She insists, in therapeutic fashion, that participants write through and about their crimes and read aloud from their texts. The film shows broken women weeping as they talk about the terrible things they have done. The writing activities showcased in the documentary are intended to empower the workshop participants, but require a perforce confessional performance that raises all the usual questions of agency inherent to colonial situations of unequal power.

Even prison writing programs that eschew statements of confession have as one of their goals the personal transformation of program enrollees. One such example is the Inside-Out Prison Exchange Program, officially launched by Lori Pompa at Temple University in 1997. By its own admission, Inside-Out is dedicated to stopping the cyclical and brutalizing effects of incarceration in the

United States by establishing a structured dialogue between "people on both sides of prison walls" that encourages participants to "discover new ways of thinking about ourselves, our society, and the systems that keep us all imprisoned" ("Breaking Down" 253). Pompa suggests a pedagogy of transformation that "leverage[s] work within one institution—the university—in order to pursue change within another—the prison" (255). The program has proven to be sustainable and replicable, with more than 7,500 inside and outside students having taken part across the United States. At the same time, this "successful" program relies on incarcerated prisoners' individual made-meanings to justify both its pedagogical and market value.

But what happens when no demonstration of individual transformation is available? If students aren't transformed, then what mechanism for purposeful critique is there? Consider these two adjacent lines from Pompa's text, the first a quote from a student in the Inside-Out program, the second Pompa's own words: "'I've emerged from the Inside-Out experience empowered with an unshakable belief in the human capacity to evolve to a higher state of social consciousness.' "The Inside-Out model of transformative pedagogy assumes that learning-with-the-whole-self lead to these kinds of epiphanies, thus supporting nothing less than the pursuit of 'a higher state of social consciousness'" ("Breaking Down" 264).

These paired comments encapsulate what Crowley calls "the inaugural gesture of metaphysics: inside/out" (*Teacher's Introduction* 11). Students are transformed along a Platonic vertical plane, their texts and interactions allowing them to move from lesser to higher states of being. While I don't question the authenticity of Inside-Out students' reflections, the program mandates that they show individual movement along a philosophical plane. For programs like Inside-Out, the rhetorical justification, if not the program focus, remains on the individual and his or her change process rather than on the collective use of writing by unconventionally constructed communities of writers.

A program that presumes a writer's highest goal to be individual transformation requires incarcerated scholars to produce texts that exemplify individual meaning-making, thereby foreclosing a critical examination of the wider enterprise. Such a program also seals off discussion of the limited meanings available to incarcerated writers (villain, hero, confessor, victim, etc.)—a narrow range of meanings that are essentially (pre)scribed. Linda Brodkey calls this type of limiting *discursive hegemony.*

In contrast, I was confronted by the myriad competing narratives of prison life in my first two days teaching at New Folsom. Some writers inside were working on Hollywood scripts that they were sure would make them famous; others penned political commentary for grassroots Bay Area publications. One writer suggested that all black inmates in California are political prisoners; another countered with a highly individualized narrative of his path to maximum security. There were stories about parents on drugs, foster care, and abuse; there were also stories about two-parent middle class families and summer vacations. The man with *FUCK YOU* tattooed in block print above his left eye gently shook my hand and wrote about his recent public performance of a traditional dance. One writer showed me pictures of his beautiful daughter, beaming as he relayed her interest in photography. He was stabbed within the year by his own gang and moved to protective custody. He was a great leader and a strong writer. I had hoped he would someday take over the class. But then he left New Folsom on a gurney. I never saw him again.

In writing about his experiences as an incarcerated teacher at High Desert State Prison, James Kilgore similarly struggles with the competing narratives he encounters while maintaining his hope that his involvement was meaningful:

> Ultimately, I am not sure if these classes were a triumph or merely a temporary respite from the ethos of hatred and violence on the yard. Definitely they were not liberatory in the Freirian sense. . . . Nonetheless . . . for me those sessions remain a cherished set of classroom moments, a series of inspiring exchanges where lights of awareness came on and the vast reservoir of wasted human potential that rests inside every prison classroom manifested itself in ways that neither the students nor myself ever previously contemplated. (49)

## SOMETHING OTHER THAN TRANSFORMATION:
### A RANGE OF AUTHORIAL PURPOSES

I have not spoken to Spoon Jackson since he was transferred from New Folsom, and I get my news of him through his blog or Twitter account. Scrolling through the posts reminds me that relationality is ever-present. Friends and supporters manage Jackson's digital space. From the blog I learn that a book of Jackson's poetry has been translated into German and that he was part of a conversation with the rapper Common on the latter's "Hope and Redemption Prison Tour." And social media isn't the only place where I can hear from Jackson: A basic search through the digital catalog of the university library returns at least four items written by him. Through Google, I can find out that the words of his essay in *By Heart*, an essay digitally published by the PEN America project that later became a chapter in his coauthored book with Judith Tannenbaum, have become the lyrics to an Ani DeFranco song. All of these threads tell the story of the relational "niche in life" that Jackson says he has created for himself.

In *Nowhere but Barstow and Prison*, Jackson writes the following:

> I sat down to breakfast my first morning in prison in a dining hall stuffed with prisoners. The noise and the mood of the place was maddening, like stepping into a huge, dark cave full of hungry bats. I could not find any familiar spot inside of myself able to relate to the bars, the concrete, and the steel, to the guns, and the guards barking out orders to hurry and eat.
>
> I was ignorant about all prison ways. I came from the desert, the natural world—purple and red clay mountains, open spaces and there was nothing natural about cells. Even the air was tainted, and twisted with unrealness, fleeting hope, and violent unrest. I was naïve, and also unconnected to any inner spirit. But my will to survive took over. I learned quickly to keep my laughter, smiles, and feelings inside and hidden behind a mask. Silence and dead-eyed frowns kept the strangers and guards at bay. (41)

In this excerpt, Jackson's search for the familiar/familial and boarding up of the soul is palpable and heart wrenching. When juxtaposed with an earlier section of the text, that which Jackson seeks—the type of niche he wants to make—becomes clearer:

> There were hardly any fences on the river bottom where we lived. The soft sands rolled under and past Blacks Bridge. Blacks Bridge was all steel with bolts like small biscuits. When I lay under the bridge, and a train ran across, I felt its power like a herd of elephants or bison stampeding across the sky. I watched the different shapes the train's shadows created on the white sands. Usually I wore no shoes so that I could feel the sands of the river as my feet sunk into them. (31)

Both of the excerpts reveal Jackson's connection to the land. The niche that Jackson is working to carve out and that may or may not result in clemency is as much about space and place as anything. Jackson isn't trying to transform or reform his soul; he is trying to re-member his connection to the sandy river bottom. A nuanced reading of the work of incarcerated writers often uncovers the type of yes/and complications found in Jackson's narrative: writing as salve *and* burden, solitude *and* relationship, transformational *and* yet not quite so.

Much of the scholarship on prison education highlights the struggle among academics to transcend colonial logics when describing the value of literacy in prison. Although relationality is present in these works, for the most part it is not closely examined, partly because it does not support disciplinary assumptions about literacy and meaning-making in texts more broadly.[3] A 2001 *English Journal* article by Gregory Shafer exemplifies a discourse that has kept the conversation on prison literacy education at the level of the individual. In his piece, Shafer tells of bringing literacy to the "dark and shadowy" halls of Coldwater Correctional Facility (75). It is clear enough throughout the piece that Shafer's intentions are good and his reading of his own experiences teaching inside are honest and earnest. Nonetheless, underlying Shafer's story is the transformational discourse so common in prison writing. Ten years later, Ed Wiltse's essay attempts to traverse the territory more carefully, yet still manages to mix important witnessing with problematic assumptions about the ability of his program to broach the prison's disciplining structures (6).

In Wiltse's program, university students can substitute a course paper for weekly book club meetings with incarcerated volunteers at Monroe Correctional Facility. This dialogic exchange is intended to complicate the university students' understanding of social problems. However, one university student's assessment of a prisoner's narrative ends with curiosity about an individual crime: "It is so crazy and makes me wonder what he is in for" (13). Such comments from university students coupled with Wiltse's own description of the program demonstrate that issues of appropriation and reification may not be as clearly settled as we might have hoped. But then there is also this beautiful statement in Wiltse's text by one of the incarcerated volunteers: "It felt good to know that every Wednesday for six weeks for at least an hour I would be able to discuss life, not self-help themes of life but life as a whole" (16). Wiltse's program, like most that I read about, is a mixed bag of valuable, life-giving opportunities for incarcerated men and women inextricably tangled with often paradoxical narratives that could easily justify arguments against implementing prison education programs.

Included in his 2013 *Radical Teacher* article "An 'Impossible Profession'? The Radical University in Prison," Atif Rafay, a student and teaching assistant in the University Beyond Bars program at the Washington State Reformatory, argues that prison course offerings can be individually agentive for incarcerated men and women. Rafay's description of what agency looks like makes room for a wide range of purposes:

> Even if many prisoners attend classes only to avoid punishment or to obtain employment credentials, or as a desperate attempt to prove themselves worthy of clemency, even if others are there merely for a pastime or for some contact with the free world, and even if the levels of academic accomplishment that most attain and the credentials they receive are mediocre, some may nonetheless learn something and perhaps even come to value learning. (12)

And yet, Rafay's comment can also be read as assuming that the incarcerated men and women who show up to class do not intrinsically value learning but rather are taught to value it by the classroom experience. Thus, even the self-proclaimed radical version of teaching in prison finds itself caught up in the discourse of transformation.

In the same issue of *Radical Teacher* as Rafay's essay, Robert Scott makes a case for setting up classrooms that are responsive to the various agentive purposes of participants without the problematic focus on transformation: "If we want to challenge the prison system in the era of mass incarceration by means of teaching college classes in prison," he writes, "we must learn how to hear the students' articulation of what is needed. We have to embrace the students' interests where they are and listen to what they need to get somewhere with their work" ("Distinguishing" 29). Implicit in Scott's call is an understanding that incarcerated men and women are doing educational work with or without the formalities of a classroom space. The idea that incarcerated people show up to class with an educational goal or project already in mind is a meaningful frame for the teacher-student relationship. It also resonates with my experience teaching incarcerated writers, all of whom brought some sense of ownership and value of the process with them to the classroom.

Eleanor Novek and Rebecca Sanford report that some writers in their prison journalism class pay "homage to loved ones on holidays or to remember family members" (117), while others seek a sense of "validation and individual attention" (118) and still others use the opportunity of writing in community to create a "'sense of normalcy'" that connects them to people and events outside of the prison (116). Ann Folwell Stanford observes that some of the women in her class "write against the official discourse of the jail, some write with it, some do both at the same time" (277) and notes that some writers bring their written work and course certificates to court appearances as demonstrations of personal growth (282). For her part, Anita Wilson reports that the consensus among the writers she worked with was that they came to class to "get away from the cockroaches" (185). From proof of transformation to a reprieve from insects, the authorial and educational purposes of incarcerated writers are as varied as the people themselves. Paying attention to the way incarcerated students describe their social needs benefits program sponsors across the political spectrum by highlighting the relational nature of much classroom work and substantiating the call to support it.

Josie Billington claims that her program distinguishes itself from other literacy interventions by making "reading a creative, social, life-enhancing activity [and] shared experience" (70). Billington also describes her program as a *therapeutic intervention*—a term problematically associated with individual transformation. Nonetheless, because she clearly articulates the relational aspect of her program, her work resonates with other scholars who teach inside (67). Novek and Sanford describe the relational needs of incarcerated students in much more intense terms: "Many female inmates write to overcome the social isolation of prison," they write. "Writing offers contact with a wider audience, meeting the visceral need for communication and supporting psychological survival" (116). A. Wilson describes her research as particularly focused on the social and the "ways that people seek to keep a sense of social identity in an institutional world" (189). In a summary of their empirical study, Halperin et al. claim that "participants benefit by being part of a social network" (10). Like Billington, Halperin et al. use a discourse of transformation—terms like *rehabilitation* and *change*—to describe their program, but their attention to the social is nonetheless significant. In each of these essays the strong need to re-member oneself as part of a social fabric is palpable.

The work of re-membering shows up clearly in the writings of Stanford, who suggests that the social purposes that incarcerated students bring to class work to form a cohesive group identity—a sense of "we"—among them. Stanford sees this making of a "we" as a form of resistance: "Often writers will begin to see themselves as a 'we' and thus subvert the individualistic rhetoric that permeates the discourse of rehabilitation and punishment," she writes. "As part of the workshop's 'we,' they also function as witnesses to each other's experience rendered through the poems" (285). By Stanford's definition, "writing that affirms a 'we' in jail is itself radical work" (291).

In describing the SpeakOut! Writers Workshops sponsored by the Community Literacy Center at Colorado State University, Jacobi nods to Stanford in suggesting that the SpeakOut! program operates on three levels, two of which pay close attention to the "we." SpeakOut! offers individuals opportunities to engage with text, but it also offers "groups of women opportunities to write and respond to writing together and often recognize their own experiences in the stories of the other writers" ("Speaking Out" 44). The program also gives participants the chance to publish their work in a biannual anthology. There exist the "we" of the classroom and the "we" of the anthology, both of which Jacobi sees as having radical potential.

Jacobi demonstrates that the work of SpeakOut! re-members incarcerated writers as an important part of communities outside the prison, and works to re-member their voices in the tapestry of pro-

Photo by Peter Merts.

gressive social movements happening beyond the prison walls. For Jacobi, the penning of counternarratives by incarcerated women forms the basis of individual *and* collective activism. These narratives function as an opening for "more ardent activism" in the individual lives of incarcerated women and also through the publication of works distributed in the community outside the prison ("Speaking Out" 41). Jacobi's attention to the way that literacy inside the prison can be dialectically responsive to "coalition-building and grassroots alliances" outside the prison manifests in a program model that works hard to put the writings of incarcerated women into circulation where they can serve outside movements. In this way, Jacobi's work highlights the possibilities for cultivating relationality between inside and outside communities.

Kirsten Coe's 2013 article on a teaching garden at Auburn Maximum Security Prison described how the identities of individual students, when brought together under the banner of a writing curriculum, can form a "we" for speaking back to power. Coe taught ecology as part of the Cornell Prison Education Program. The twenty-one students in the course used a 50' × 100' converted green space as a field site. Coe relates the experience of watching a guard heckle the students as they were being escorted from the teaching garden to the school building on one of the final days of the course: "So what are you guys now? Farmers, weed growers?" he asked sarcastically. "No," one of the students responded. "We are ecologists" (60).

Coe's story is instructive for folks who intend to teach inside. Although she is more ready than I would be to ascribe to it a transformational outcome, she nonetheless describes an educational scenario where students are invited to join a collective status—that of ecologists—that was not available to them before the teaching garden was established. That group status becomes agentive as it literally gives the student words with which to speak back to the adversarial guard.

The following excerpt from Ann Folwell Stanford's 2004 article shows how her critical self-reflection and attention to student articulations of needs led to concrete improvements to her program:

It tapped into my concern that I was offering only palliative moments and, in so doing, actually supporting and making the very system of which I am so critical actually look good. My acute awareness of privilege as a white middle-class academic, free to come and go in this enclosed space, added to my unease and growing sense of collusion (this issue alone warrants a separate article). Instead of the one-time sessions, I switched formats and began holding workshops that lasted four to six weeks per tier. Although this obviously did not resolve the issue of racial and class privilege or of collusion with the system, it did offer participants some continuity and the opportunity to create a body of work. (281)

Stanford doesn't ascribe to the classroom experience any grand transformation. What she does describe—some continuity and some opportunity for sustained projects—appears to be important to the incarcerated students. This responsiveness to the "we" of the classroom is what makes her move to longer-format sessions important.

In a similar vein, Scott suggests that prison programs must attend to the articulated social purposes of students and calls for increasingly fluid and open classroom models: "If we are determined to have liberatory pedagogy in prison, it will have to proceed in an un-deterministic manner," he writes. "That means abandoning vanguardist proselytizing for the left, and being open to the possibility that the most important lesson from the college course can be in the dynamics of interaction between the classroom participants" ("Distinguishing" 26). The writings of both Stanford and Scott reflect a reoccurring tension between ethics, ideals, and the material constraints of working inside the near-totalizing carceral institution. Both writers respond to this tension by describing classrooms that are structured flexibly enough to respond to the expressed needs of students.

Classrooms with a seemingly loose structure have been criticized from the outside as forms of institutional placation as well as from the inside by those who come to class expecting disciplinary rigor packaged in a traditional teacher-student power dynamic. Of course, a positive relational pedagogy is no more at odds with high-quality curriculum than it is synonymous with a voyeuristic teaching experience. The goal of a relational pedagogy is to use the rigor and content of the classroom to strengthen existing relationships while developing opportunities to reframe "how we might regard and relate to one another" (Jacobi, "Curating" 115).

Beyond listening for and responding to the diversity of reasons students come to class, attending to the "we" of the classroom requires critical self-reflection on the part of the teacher. Jacobi addresses the dangers of activist teachers misunderstanding the limits of their roles while also failing to acknowledge their complicity in working within and against carceral institutions. Likewise, Jacobi and Becker make it clear that the role of the writing teacher should not be conflated or erroneously expanded beyond its bounds:

> Facilitators are not social workers, correctional guards, substance abuse counselors, or parole officers. We are not in the business of addiction recovery, public safety, family reunification, or even conventional education, though our efforts may complement work in those areas. As we have indicated, our focus on literacy and particularly written expression, craft an alternative publication along with our grounding in feminist and queer pedagogy creates a commitment to the written word as active participant in progressive social justice and grassroots organizing movements. (37)

A prison scholar-teacher with an activist orientation who can understand and maintain her primary "commitment to the written word" is walking a tightrope. As Eric Cummins relates in his history of California's radical prison movement between 1950 and 1980, the relational interplay between community activists and incarcerated writer/activists can be fraught. When and where it ends in bloodshed, it is almost always the blood of incarcerated men and women that is spilt. And even when it does not result in violence against incarcerated men and women, the potential for manipulation and appropriation, or at least misunderstanding, is always present.

The collection of essays highlighted here demonstrates that relational purposes for education have already been articulated by incarcerated students, and that some scholar-teachers in the prison are recognizing those purposes and actively working to support them. Yet the work of operating inside and against systems in which we are complicit is deeply complicated. Jacobi and Becker's warnings about misunderstanding the boundaries of the role of teacher and Cummins's history of blatant appropriation strongly suggest that more is needed than a sympathetic or activist spirit. To move beyond good intentions, ethically sound and relationally oriented structural frames are needed. For the most part, a gap remains in the scholarship when it comes to articulating the institutional structures that can create and maintain classrooms in which incarcerated students have real agency in the work of re-membering and where scholar-teachers operate in ways that are respectful, relational, and reciprocal without crossing lines that endanger students or programs.

## RELATIONALITY IN THE HISTORY
## OF ARTS IN CORRECTIONS

Arts in Corrections, as articulated by its founders, was a program oriented around an ethic of opportunity. From the beginning, the focus of the program was on bridging the relational distance between the inside and outside of the prison by offering students a range of artistic educational opportunities taught by professional artists from the outside. The regular involvement of these teaching artists across the state did open the doors to the prison a bit wider, both physically and metaphorically.

The performance of *Waiting for Godot* by incarcerated students at San Quentin is one notable example: Six hundred community members from outside the prison were escorted in for three performances. Another example is the series of three performances of an oratorio hosted by AIC students at New Folsom for approximately 250 community members.[4] At the request of the public audiences who attended the inside performances, a recording of the oratorio was professionally mixed and produced by Henry Robinett, a Sacramento-based jazz musician and record producer. Because the musicians could not come downtown to Robinett's studio, he brought the studio to them: AIC staff transformed one of the classrooms into a recording studio for an entire week so that the incarcerated musicians could professionally record the music that they had arranged themselves. One thousand copies of the oratorio were distributed free of charge to the community with the support of private donors. This example shows the value of community-oriented projects centered around the contributions of incarcerated participants and highlights again the "we" that is so often a sustaining force in prison classrooms.

These projects were born into a tightly woven and well-tended web of relations. Both the story of *Godot* and Robinett's pop-up recording studio include mountains of memos and institutional back-channel work by Carlson in his role as artist facilitator. Neither of these projects would have come to life without an institutional insider capable of bending existing structures and, in so doing, re-creating them. That work, as Carlson described it, was unequivocally relational. A time-lapse film of either of those endeavors would have shown him traversing the yard, ping-ponging between the offices of the warden, the facility captain, the public relations officer, and the community resources manager. Clearing institutional, relational pathways is tedious, incremental work; the memo to bring in a rope for the performance of *Godot* was preceded by memos requesting paper and pencil one year, juggling balls the next, and so on. In this way, Carlson, and other AIC artist facilitators, built a legacy in which the space of possibility, though in a constant state of expansion and contractions, generally grew. It was into that physical and relational space that I stepped in 2009.

A close consideration of all the relations that animated the California AIC program between 1980 and 2003 requires attention to not just people and place but also the historical moment in which Arts in Corrections emerged. Here again I am thinking of V. F. Cordova's claim that "present actions are like layers of snow added to a snowball—the shape of the present outer layer determines the future shape of the whole" (175). The shape of the prevailing attitudes and theories of "correction" present at the inception of the AIC program provided an opening between waves of more positivistic theories of "correction" that allowed programs like AIC to form. Prior ideological ruptures in the status quo are instructive in this regard. According to Stephen Duguid, theory and research in psychology and biology inspired the medical explanations of deviance that dominated those fields between roughly 1949 and 1977 despite a lack of evidence for the efficacy of such models (244). Decades of close study and treatment of deviants passed without much, if any, notable progress toward a cure, leading Robert Martinson to write the following in 1976:

> It may be that there is a radical flaw in our present strategies—that education at its best, or that psychotherapy at its best, cannot overcome, or even appreciably reduce, the powerful tendency for offenders to continue in criminal behavior. Our present treatment programs are based on a theory of crime as a disease—that is to say, as something foreign and abnormal in the individual which cannot presumably be cured. This theory may well be flawed, in that it overlooks—even denies—both the normality of crime in society and the personal normality of a very large proportion of offenders, criminals who are merely responding to the facts and conditions of our society. ("California" 190)

In leveling his critique, Martinson opened up a small window through which the sociologist reentered the conversation. What emerged was the opportunities model, which more or less adhered to the idea that incarcerated people could and would make choices about their own transformation if given the space and tools with which to do so. Duguid notes that, beginning in the 1970s, prisons moved away from a medical model to the opportunities model by collaborating with private and public entities to offer a range of activities and programs aimed at meeting needs, including but not limited to "recreation, education, training, counseling or therapy." Although the opportunity model was rooted in the idea of individual transformation, it nonetheless opened up some rhetorical space in which to challenge the subject-object orientation of the medical model.

By the 1990s, US prisons had experienced a severe return to the medical model and stripped away many of the sponsored programs that had been allowed to develop in the previous two decades (Duguid 247). But while the opportunity model was in fashion, programs across North America saw a purposeful rearticulation of incarcerated people as agentive subjects—students, learners, actors, writers, and so on—operating, to some extent, in ways of their own choosing. In response to this definitional revision of incarcerated people, programs emerged that were "complex in nature, multi-faceted, attempted to address a variety of needs and desires, and were grounded in institutions and affiliations outside the bureaucratic orbit of the criminal justice system" (247). Duguid notes that the locus of program sponsorship was often outside the Department of Corrections and thus "opened up the prison system to outsiders," resulting in programs that "were often messy, untidy, chaotic but seldom if ever disastrous" (253).

To an extent, subversive and progressive activities were allowed to operate under the opportunities model alongside those that more closely tracked the individualistic and reformatory ideology of the prison system. These programs worked to counter the notion of prisoner as object, linked directly and often to the outside community, and spanned a wide range of activities. They made use of "democratic ethics, a diverse set of political linkages, and an inevitably complex set of needs and relations" (Duguid 251). To my knowledge, nowhere in the record of AIC is the program described as following the opportunity model as outlined by Duguid. But it fit the model's contours: it offered a wide range of choices, employed participatory management styles, encouraged attendees to assume agentive identities, eschewed coercion, relied on attendees to maintain order, fostered meaningful relationships with the outside community, and established shared models of sponsorship at least partially outside the prison (247).

The AIC program was made possible by its connection to a few significant public universities and at least one strong political ally. Initially, the program grew out of the University of California, Los Angeles ArtsReach grant, and its champion at the William James

Association was Eloise Smith, who brought along her political connections to University of California at Santa Cruz and Senator Henry Mello, who became a reliable friend of the program. The initial links between prison and university loosened as other entities entered the web of relations responsible for creating and sustaining AIC during its thirty-year run. Nevertheless, university sponsorship played a key instigative role.

None of this history sounds decolonial and none of AIC's many sponsors describe it in such terms. Nevertheless, the story of AIC includes moments that resonate with decolonial practice as described by Ndlovu-Gatsheni and Zondi, particularly in the way that it created, at least temporarily, some space for agency and choice among participants. It is worth noting that the pilot Prison Arts Project at Vacaville came as a response to an invitation Smith received from incarcerated artists looking for professional instruction to support the art community they had already created for themselves. She accepted that invitation and went to Vacaville to learn about and support their work. This origin story provides evidence of a structure built both in response to and in community with local articulations of need.

Michel Wenzer's 2011 documentary *At Night I Fly* showcases some of the politically unprecedented ways in which the AIC space at New Folsom stretched and sometimes even ruptured expected ways of being in the prison. In the film, an associate warden sits in the AIC room talking to Spoon Jackson and Marty Williams. The conversation is honest, with both Jackson and Williams directly challenging the idea that the associate warden is trying to communicate. The dialectical back and forth between the three men stands in stark contrast to the more typical vignettes between keeper and the kept available in both the literature on prison and in representations from popular culture. The associate warden's participation in the project implicates him in the film's critique of mass incarceration in the United States—a significant political risk he was willing to take.

Clearly, relationally extraordinary things can happen in prison. Of course, the widespread human rights violations and the more mundane horrors of life behind bars do not disappear, for me, in some rosy glow behind a handful of local, agentive interactions. But these interactions are important and instructive for teachers inside even if they do not augur revolution. Ruptures in the relational status quo, such as between racial groups or between incarcerated people and custodial staff, point again to the need to find ways to pay attention to and account for the relational aspects of life inside even the most totalizing institutions. The associate warden from the film did not participate in heartfelt conversations with incarcerated teaching artists on his first day. But he did start as a member of the custody staff that oversaw the day-to-day operations of AIC. Through that process, he had the chance to build relationships with practitioners and incarcerated participants and in so doing gain a respect for the program that informed his choice many years later to take on the political risk of hosting a film crew, allowing himself to be filmed in an intellectual tussle with incarcerated participants, and facilitating a level of institutional access that surprised all involved.

Beyond respectful and productive relations with custodial staff, the specific and strategic relational chemistry of AIC at New Folsom also allowed for varied and sustained opportunities for incarcerated students to disrupt the prison status quo regarding inmate self-sufficiency. Both the program and its participants operated inside the prison with a relatively high degree of autonomy. As the program gained credibility inside the institution, access to quality teaching and materials continued to grow. What emerged was a delicately maintained space for rich interaction and learning where incarcerated participants took on significant roles as both teachers and administrators, working with folks from outside the prison in unprecedented collaboration.

Highlighting the qualities of choice, participatory management, and community contact does not imply that the program was without fault. The individual experiences of AIC, for both students and teachers, varied in the same ways that all classroom experiences vary. What is of consequence here is the fact that the AIC room at New Folsom operated for seventeen years without major incident (Carlson). Incarcerated students were able to operate, to an extent, in ways of their own choosing because they followed the rules and tended the institutional relationships that affected the program's basic existence. The AIC room became a safe space for experimentation with some of the defining mores of the institution—namely, the rules that govern conversations across race and power.

A scene from the 2011 documentary shows a racially mixed group of AIC participants having a honest and heated conversation about race politics on the yard. Conversations about race, and conversations across race, are hard to broker at New Folsom, where sustained racial violence dictates much of the day-to-day operations of the place. For example, there was a long stretch of time when AIC students affiliated with certain gangs were required by gang code to instigate violence whenever they crossed paths with members of a rival gang. For this reason, gang-affiliated students had to attend class on alternating days, creating some disjointedness. As another example: At one point, all black inmates, even those were not gang-affiliated, were locked down for almost a year in response to a gang-related incident. So when the racially mixed group of AIC participants in *At Night I Fly* talk about yard politics, the implications of such an act are as serious as the heated conversation suggests. However, as evidenced in the film, unprecedented things like heated conversations about race that do not end in violence can and do happen, and such relational ruptures are worth noting and learning from.

It is important to note that there is a distinction "between alternatives to the system of domination and oppression and alternatives within the same system" (Santos 78). The story of AIC more broadly (and the particular bits of that story shared here) are stories of alternatives *within* rather than alternatives *to*. No amount of revisionist history changes that. Nonetheless, these bits of history provide an important counternarrative of the prison, showing it to be a decidedly more organic and relational place than generally portrayed. When I hear prison scholar-teachers frantically defend the need to traffic in narratives of transformation or make use of economic logics to defend the existence of their programs, I remember James Baldwin's words: "The world is before you and you need not take it or leave it as it was when you came in." If Baldwin is right, and I think he is, then it is important to circulate the counternarratives that paint a more nuanced and relational, and therefore accurate, portrait of the systems of domination and oppression for which we seek alternatives.

## TOWARD DECOLONIAL OPTIONS AND RELATIONAL METHODOLOGIES

In his posthumously published collection of essays *I Write What I Like,* Steve Biko, the South African antiapartheid activist who died in police custody in 1977, addresses the issue of relationality and relational accountability in the context of the antiapartheid struggle, speaking directly to the role of the intellectual in the fight for freedom. When I read his critique of the ways that well-meaning white liberals injected themselves into the movement without a reflective consideration of their race and class positions, I hear him speaking directly to prison scholar-teachers:

> We are concerned with that curious bunch of nonconformists who explain their participation in negative terms: that bunch of do-gooders that goes under all sorts of names—liberals, leftists, etc. These are the people who argue that they are not responsible for white racism and the country's "inhumanity to the black man." These are the people who claim that they too feel the oppression just as acutely as the blacks and therefore should be jointly involved in the black man's struggle for a place under the sun. (20)

Biko suggests that mutual respect is foundational to any lasting antiapartheid effort: "Once the various groups within a given community have asserted themselves to the point that mutual respect has to be shown then you have the ingredients for a true and meaningful integration" (21), he writes. The mutual respect that Biko describes is built on relational accountability. In accountable relationships, all parties have the ability to speak, listen, and move in ways of their own choosing. Where outsiders presume insider positions, the possibility of mutual respect and productive relationship is lost. Biko's criticism is helpful in pointing out that allyship requires more that an individual, emotional commitment to righting a wrong.

Intellectuals committed to the hard work of reflecting on and recognizing their own subject positions and then, from there, moving to build respectful and reciprocal relationships can and should commit themselves to addressing the myriad social-historical issues at hand. Surely mass incarceration in the United States is a pressing social issue deserving such attention. Those of us in the field of composition must take a long look at the ways in which our research methodologies still carry a colonial sensibility that works against an overarching disciplinary rhetoric and intention. This long view of history should particularly inform our impatient impulse to demonstrate that literacy has material value for the individual, and especially so in places like prison, where the material benefits of writing are scarce and the potential for punishment is ever present, as Dylan Rodríguez has pointed out. Furthermore, the myriad authorial purposes of writers in the prison classroom suggest a need to carefully (re)consider what it is we think we know about the prison classroom and how we can reasonably demonstrate it.

As with other contemporary crises, the issue of what to do with the over seven million people caught up in the US prison system may not be served by a master agenda. What may be more helpful are reciprocal relationships and a purposeful disbanding of the ethics and rhetorics of transformation. Between committed composition teachers and a practice that ethically supports their intention lie important epistemological and structural questions about how to support the "we" of the prison classroom, what counts as valuable in those pursuits, and how such value can be studied and demonstrated.

Whenever we write about prison programs, we are writing into and out of paradox. I do not expect that I will ever find the right words with which to describe both what I witness when I teach inside and what I want to see on the scholarly horizon. But I know that I would like to forward university-sponsored projects that work to re-member incarcerated students as members of existing communities, and I see that such work requires methodologies grounded in respect, responsibility, reciprocity, and relationality. The conversation about how to build and enact such methodologies is taken up in the next chapter.

# WRITERS AND TEACHERS, PART 3

**1st Yard**

This is a true story.

It's 11:15 on a beautiful, clear May morning. Unseasonably cool perhaps, but the perfect weather for a barbeque in the backyard, a picnic with someone special. But I shut this out because my imagination runs off and collides with my reality.

I awoke five hours earlier with the same strange mixture of unfocused expectancy and gnawing boredom as I had every morning for the previous five weeks. Although I had just got to prison and had yet to fully adjust, I felt like this feeling would never go away. I got up, washed in silence, and ate breakfast with all the usual excitement of Oliver Twist—soft food for hard men.

But by 11:15, it's time for Yard. My first Yard. My first Yard in a Level IV prison.

My cellie is anxious. He's a "reg"—a regular—someone who's been around and knows his shit. I watch as he fidgets with a pencil, first starting to write a short note then stopping, thinking, writing some more. I see him lost in thought, making decisions about the next 90 minutes of his life. If he's anxious, then I'm fucked.

I am trying, somewhat successfully, to learn everything I can from everything he does and even more importantly, everything he does not do. I try to pick up on every detail and file them away without making it obvious that all I've really been able to master at this point is keeping my mouth shut. I fail. I want to ask a million questions. I feel like I'll never run out of those, but my cellie isn't the answering type. He didn't ask to be saddled with a new-boot, an untested and unblooded youngster, a total unknown, and he doesn't even try to hide his resentment at my arrival.

I watch as he organizes his property, grouping items together— those he hopes to keep and those he doesn't care about, much. "Just in case," he mutters over his shoulder to the curious dependent he knows is looking on. "Just in case," I silently intone.

Once it's my turn on the floor, I don't quite know what to do with myself. I feel like I should wash up again, as I'm already sweating. It's not at all hot in the cell, but icy beads have begun to form on my back and sides all the same. I decide this is a ridiculous thing to do just before going outside in the official "Exercise Yard." But even so, I try to remember what my cellie did to prepare for . . . well, whatever is coming next. Did I hear the water running? Did I see him over there? I settle for putting on too many state-issued clothes and then set about tying and re-tying my boots, like that matters.

11:15 and the doors are opening.

11:15 and one hundred twenty-eight slivers of fear and angst come striding out the Yard Door, off to face whatever is going to happen, most of which they can barely control. 11:15 and every Block on the Yard opens their doors, as their same one twenty-eight walk on into the sunlight and the unknown. 11:15 and it's an impossibly beautiful May morning. We all try our best to block out that inner voice telling us to run, to hide, trying to ignore the sinking stomachs and leaden feet. We focus instead on the task at hand—shoving aside our better selves to keep one foot moving in front of the other.

The Yard is so much larger than I imagined, but made all the more compact and volatile by 700 angry men jockeying for space to temporarily plant their flags, until roughly five armed camps spring to life. Nobody talks to me, nobody tells me the rules. I get a few hard-eyed chin dips and a lot of curious glances, some with tight smiles I mistake for humor. I feel like a country boy on his first trip to New York City, gawking at all the foreign sights and smells. But I try not to look too long at any one person, any one thing, lest I give away my inexperience and fragility. I fail.

Suddenly it occurs to me that my cellie is gone. Up and vanished while I was busy showing off my youth. *Fuck.* The one thing he told me to make sure I did was to keep near him and not let him out of my sight. One fucking instruction finally, grudgingly given, and I immediately forgot. *Fuck.*

I look around quickly, doing my best to not seem panicked or frightened, while simultaneously broadcasting both for the entire Yard to see. My head is on a swivel, the very action that makes it look to anyone watching, and therefore *everyone out here*, that you are nervous and worried about some threat you imagine is coming your way. Not good. I start to remember some instruction I once knew, probably from a movie about war fittingly enough, to breathe. Scan and breathe, breathe and scan. Starting to settle down, I begin my survey of the Yard through clearer eyes. Left and right, back and forth, breathe, scan, breathe, scan, breathe. Finally, I see him off a little ways with four other toughs, solemnly discussing the fate of their worlds. Instantly relieved, I start to feel a little less worried that everything I'm seeing also escapes my sight. Breathe and scan, scan and breathe.

And that is when it happens—so fast, I see it as small vignettes of slow motion.

I catch a quick, focused movement to my left. A purposeful walk, predator eyes forward, right hand clenching something low. Then, a sudden burst of motion—up, left and straight back, then turning right and away. A shout of surprise. A hand up to the neck. A burst of red mist coloring the cool blue sky. Superfluous questions asked and I hear, clearly, "What'd I do?!" as though it matters.

More movement, over there, to the right. A third person in motion jumping up from his perch by the track to slash and plunge, his knife piercing flesh and a man goes down. All is red and blue. Denim jackets, shirts, jeans, and blood spread out on the ground as the P.A. horn bellows, "DOWN ON THE YARD!!" Panicked gurgling as blood flows and muffled nervous laughter as it spreads. Suppressed hysteria. Now shouting, running, combat boots thundering on asphalt, keys jingling on leather belts and metal clubs in hand, forever at the ready. A gurney arrives with medical Staff and shouts for more pressure. The gurney surges by, and all eyes watch as blood smacks the ground all the way to the clinic.

Cops *everywhere*, more than I thought even worked here and all of them ordering something different. But curiously enough, the tension leaves the Yard like fog burning off in the late morning sun as everyone falls into the familiar routine of strip-outs right where you lie. Groups of naked men on the basketball court, the running track, handball courts and baseball diamond. *Everywhere.* The cloying scent of fear and dirty clothes permeating the air. Shriveled dicks and bad tattoos. Now I'm up and it's all happening so fast: shirt, pants, boxers, socks; bend over, cough, nope, do it again; clothes back on and not fitting right; double time it back to the cellblock with the relief it wasn't me but the fear that another incident might happen before I get back. Why did that happen? What did he do? I want to know everything so I can learn how to keep my blood on the inside.

The cell door shuts with a satisfying clunk, paradoxically signifying the greatest little piece of safety I will ever have. My cellie, the "reg," my frustratingly quiet and quietly threatening source of information, got swept up in the investigation and taken to the hole. I'm nineteen years old as I sit on my bunk alone in the cell and think about what my life has become.

My mind starts a conversation with itself that extends out for many years: "That just happened. This is real. I must learn. I must change. I will not die here; not here, not alone." Later that night I will lie awake for a long, long time as I imagine a different reality. A better day in May.

—Adam Hinds

## Guntower Homily

Raised Catholic, his mind slips back
To catechism class
To the Sixth Commandment
    *thou shalt not kill*
it seemed the clearest of them all
most easily obeyed,
until three minutes ago.

The yard below him churns with men,
faces from light to dark
their bodies clad in prison denims and greys,
and they swirl together,
stain each other crimson
their knives striking falling rising
they scramble and charge again.

His correctional training has taught him to target the aggressors,
to target those who wield the weapons,
those inflicting wounds on the others,
the others unable to defend themselves.

He hesitates.
    What does it mean to kill?
    Is is permissible to kill in order to prevent a killing?
    What if each man appears intent on killing the other?

Too many questions.

He recites the Hail Mary
    (full of grace)
    and fires a quick succession—
    three rounds into the concrete, splintering and spraying

letting trajectory and chance, letting God make the decision.
                     —Michael L. Owens

From *The Way Back* by Mike Owens. Random Lane Press © 2017. Reprinted by permission.

## Year of Jubilee

<u>Winter:</u>

It is a mild January and the tulips start to come up. But memory tells me there will be two more months of ice, followed by mud and wind. I worry about the fate of the early tulips.

I also worry about Buddy, who lives in Alaska, writes and sings folk songs, paints houses to get by and will die before Spring's green points push all the way up through the soil. He already went inside the prison to say good-bye and exchange last songs. All that is left is bedside prayer, sheets soaked through with the cold sweat of in between, familiar candlelit faces, a rattling birdbreast and silence.

Buddy is passing, taking with him some of Marty and the Golden Age of Arts in Corrections that saw a steady string of volunteer musicians coming to C Facility from a dozen states. They began stepping off of tour buses and out of borrowed cars, many of them at the urging of Buddy. The first time Buddy came in he spent two hours with a handful of serious guitarists. He was impressed, visibly shaken, unwilling to talk about the experience. At lunch afterwards—seven miles outside the front gate—Buddy pulled a folded stack of bills out of his pocket, stained and smelling of cigarettes: $240.00. It was all the money he had made the night before at a gig in Nevada City. "Do the guys have any Bob Dylan?" Buddy asked Jim. "They need to listen to Bob Dylan. Buy the guys some Dylan."

Jim learned of Buddy from a C Facility doctor who listens to KMVR Grass Valley. The doctor thought the guys inside could relate to Buddy's work: songs like "Medicated Family" and "Jesus Love Me More Than He Loves You." Jim called the station. They called Buddy. Buddy came down from Alaska. Met Marty. Wrote "Year of Jubilee." Sang it one last time six years later when he came to say good-bye:

> "Razor wire stretched across the open sky
> Some of you will walk out
> Some will fly
> Upwards towards the brightness of the sun
> And leave behind forever
> The things that you have done."

<u>Spring:</u>

By March, it is already hot, and the morning sun bakes the concrete. I am waiting to teach class, standing outside the art room in the chain-link prison-style front porch where Spoon used to feed the birds. Jim suggests that Marty helped Buddy process Cancer and come to terms with dying. I turn to Marty, eyes wide.

"Marty, you gave Buddy permission to die?" I mean the question with respect, take seriously the honor of walking a friend down a last road.

Marty takes a quick step back. "I would not say that," he says. We keep talking. The conversation works its way down to the question that matters, the one Marty asked Buddy, the one that finally gave Buddy rest.

"Is it enough?"

—Anna Plemons

# 3

## Toward Relational Methodologies: Learning from the Work of Indigenous Scholars

> The enemy of the incarcerated also lurks in us, not only when we come abusively—to study the criminal mind, to enhance our resumes, to get a grade, to be cool, to feel good about—but also when we are careless, immature, disrespectful, unprofessional, treating our enemy with hostility, our friends with disregard.
> —William Alexander, *Is William Martinez Not Our Brother?*

> Post-colonial? There is nothing post about it. It has simply shape-shifted to fit the contemporary context.
> —Margaret Kovach, *Indigenous Methodologies*

SPEAKING AS THE PRESIDENT OF THE Saskatchewan Indian Federated College, Eber Hampton suggests that "memory comes before knowledge"—that is, that scholars need to remember why they are asking the questions they are asking and be clear about the motivations of their research (48). When I look back over my first years teaching at New Folsom and simultaneously working to join the discipline of composition, I can see how my disciplining pulled me toward an empirical focus on the individual while my memories at the prison kept confirming that the classroom landscape could not quite fit into that disciplinary frame. And the more I looked around, the more I found that other scholars were speaking to this disequilibrium, taking half-steps and making false starts but never quite sidestepping the coloniality at the root of our most closely held disciplinary ideas. In this chapter, I trace the outline of some of the Indigenous scholarship that helped me to understand the prison as a relational space that could benefit from a relational methodology. The chapter concludes with a proposed relational methodology for prison scholar-teachers aligned with the work of Margaret Kovach.

## BECOMING DISCIPLINED, ENTERING COLONIALITY

As I've already mentioned, when I first volunteered at New Folsom in 2009, I was a guest teacher in the classrooms of Spoon Jackson and Marty Williams, both of whom are serving life without the possibility of parole sentences. They are both really good teachers and their non-credit-bearing classes had long waiting lists despite the fact that joining such writing groups is complicated by the prison-yard politics of race. Many writers in the AIC program defied strict racial lines and gang affiliations to collaborate in community, challenging the dehumanizing structures of incarceration that position incarcerated people as color-coded, numerically organized bodies.

I realized quickly that Jackson and Williams had much to add to the conversation about writing pedagogy. The compelling nature of their work and the layered affordances of the classroom space they had helped create inspired me to pursue a doctorate. I had hoped to support what they were doing and help bring the conversation I was having with these two teachers into the public discourse about teaching. But when I began my doctoral program, I became a representative (for better or worse) of my university, and I quickly learned that the conversation I had been attempting to facilitate between people inside and outside the prison suddenly required the review and permission of my academic institution.

Since my relationship with Jackson and Williams preceded my work at the university by more than two years, I did not see them as objects of study but rather as teaching colleagues with exceedingly limited agency, yet the IRB process required me to consider them subjects and outline how I intended to study them. It also demanded that I confine my study to a preauthorized, linear time period. What I had learned from my relationship with Jackson and Williams before January 2012 or after January 2013 had to be left out of the record. And then there was the matter of anonymity. I had originally hoped to film Jackson and Williams talking about their experience as teachers and include such film in conference discussions on pedagogy. The idea of filming Jackson and Williams made sense to me at the time because I did not want to speak for these teachers and hoped that the filming project would allow them, in a limited way, to speak for themselves.

From the start, my project was based on intertwined and mutually exclusive logics—I wanted Jackson and Williams to enter the scholarly discourse about teaching writing, but the scholarly discourse that I thought needed their voices required a perforce constraining of them as objects of a linear, time-based, and preferably anonymous study to whom I would need to describe the risks of participation and for whom I would need to have an institutionally preapproved set of questions. The list of vague questions that I finally submitted to the IRB included the following statement, which makes no sense to me whatsoever even though I wrote it:

> The following discussion items have been identified as the intended focus of the Creative Arts Program ethnographic work. It is understood that these themes will be introduced, but that participants will have the freedom to respond in ways that appropriately widen that context. However, the ethnographic work will continually be constrained to dialogue that meets the conditions outlined in the IRB in that risks will be commensurate with those acceptable to nonprison volunteers (language from Addendum 3).

I don't know how it could be humanly possible to constrain dialogue in ways that ensure risks to incarcerated people resemble risks to people outside the prison. Even outside the prison, the risks to human subjects in conversation cannot entirely be known, and it is pure hubris for scholars like myself to guess after or promise safety in the exchanging of words. Such a claim evokes the critique of Scott Momaday, who writes: "We have no being beyond our stories. Our stories explain us, justify us, sustain us, humble us, and forgive us. And sometimes they injure and destroy us. Make no mistake, we are at risk in the presence of words" (169).

Events at the prison in 2012 further complicated the project, leading me to see clearly the need for study designs that respect and can account for the complex and relational nature of prison work. In 2012 the California Department of Corrections began "reevaluating points" for all persons serving life without parole (LWOP) sentences. In the context of prison, higher points correspond to higher levels of restriction and surveillance. The prior system had set a numeric floor on the assessment of points for LWOP inmates, guaranteeing that they could not work themselves, through good behavior, down to Level 3 institutions. In 2011 the US Supreme Court ruled that overcrowding in the California prison system constituted a violation of the Eighth Amendment's ban on cruel and unusual punishment. In response, the State decided to reevaluate the point structure that determines the movement of incarcerated people between individual institutions in California's four-tiered prison system.

One major piece of that state-level restructuring was the lowering of the floor on LWOP points. This process forced Jackson and Williams to leave the maximum-security prison that offered the paid clerking posts allowing them to run AIC and teach writing and music classes, which they had been doing for some fifteen and thirteen years respectively. I did not resubmit my 2011 IRB application, because I had already gone inside to say good-bye to these two men who were being forced to leave work that was important to them and to the people who attended their classes. The situation was distressing for both teaching artists. Additionally, Williams, who is white, was in serious danger of disciplinary violence from other white inmates at his next prison because of his choice to live and teach on a yard with a "soft white line"—prison-speak for places where white inmates have chosen to live peaceably with incarcerated people of color.

One of the questions on the IRB "Continuing Review" form asked me to "describe any additional risks or benefits observed during the course of the study." Although the risks to Williams in the move to Level 3 have nothing to do with my study, I could not stomach asking a man who was worried about his bodily safety in an unwelcome move to a new institution to sign an abstract consent form outlining the risks of participation in our ongoing conversation. Because I did not ask Jackson and Williams to sign "Continuing Review" consent forms, the study was terminated and I received this notification:

> This notice is to let you know that the human subject project titled "Arts in Corrections Ethnography" (IRB #12147) was last approved on 1/26/2012 and the IRB approval has expired on 1/25/2013. The study has become inactive. Data collection and participant recruitment must be suspended. Any further data collection from human research participants will require reactivation and/or resubmission of the full application.

I understand and respect the role of the IRB and even currently serve on the review board at the university where I teach. Nonetheless, this notice highlights the problems that arose from my initially agreeing to consider Jackson and Williams objects of study about whom I was collecting data. I had agreed to those institutional and disciplinary terms for two reasons. First, I imagined that the benefits to the scholarly discourse would outweigh the drawbacks. Second, I did not see that there were any options for working with Jackson and Williams that would not require this setup. In the end, I did not film Jackson or Williams talking about their teaching experience because it seemed like an insensitive and arbitrary way to spend what little time they had left at New Folsom.

But then, neither Jackson nor Williams was moved right away. As they waited for the promised "reevaluation of points," they continued teaching. We continued talking about pedagogy. All of the conversations and events that occurred between the termination of my study and Jackson and Williams being transferred contributed to my understanding of relationality in the prison system, and there is not a way for me to mentally bracket off the knowledge I gained during the one year of IRB approval from the before and after of my collegial relationship with Jackson and Williams.

I am not the first prison teacher-scholar to find that the structures of study sanctioned by my university presume a "chronological lie" (Bosworth; Cohen and Taylor). As Downes and Rock have pointed out, the un-truth of arbitrary start and end dates in the study of ongoing programs allows researchers to imagine that their questions emerge systematically from a tightly framed theory; that their research begins and ends on schedule; and that they are able to take that clean and closed data set back to their offices to "ponder and amend the theory that fathered it." My own experiences of talking and working with Jackson and Williams before and after my sanctioned study reaffirms the impossibility of designing a sterilized, linear study of prison writing practices and led me to look for theories of writing that can account for the relational complexity present in the prison writing classroom without dismissing—or dis-membering—the broader relational and chronological context.

Although Jackson and Williams did eventually board buses for other prisons, the community of writers at New Folsom remained, doing what it always does to stay alive. While hyper-focusing on including Spoon and Marty, via video, in the broad, academic conversation about prison arts happening on campus, I missed the opportunity to listen to the community that remained and support their tending of the writing space through processes of reorganization. I could have asked the remaining community of writers questions about how their community functioned; how they used writing for personal, local, and extra-institutional purposes; what they thought they might need as the shape of AIC at New Folsom was changing; and how folks like me might marshal resources to ease that transition for them.

My focus on individual authors distracted me from the broader work of fostering respectful, responsible, and reciprocal relationships with the *entire* community of writers. To be clear, framing the prison classroom as an organic, relational space does not directly translate to respectful, responsible, and reciprocal relationships between the scholar and the writing community. And the story of my attempted study fits easily into a mostly unwritten record of activist scholar-teachers misunderstanding—or worse, abusing—their relationship with incarcerated writers. Nonetheless, recognizing the organic and relational reality of the prison classroom does begin to move a scholar-teacher toward potentially decolonial frames, or decolonial options in Mignolo's terms. With that said, I am not the first scholar-teacher in the prison to miss an opportunity to respectfully listen and reciprocally respond to the classroom community.

A few years ago, I sat around the table at a national conference talking with other teachers who work in or write about the US prison. One scholar called for a closer attention to the ethical complications of teaching in prison and publishing on that work. In response, another participant suggested that a monograph she was working on might be harmful to the incarcerated people with whom she had worked,[1] but cited the IRB as the sole functionary standing between her and her ability to have respectful, reciprocal relationships with the incarcerated writers. In this exchange, I saw clearly how transformational rhetorics both authorize and subsume the particular coloniality between the "knower" and the "known," obscuring for educators the fact that they are responsible for the very things they imagine they are disrupting. The scholar at our table was willing to put incarcerated people in physical jeopardy in the service of a text that she determined needed publishing. Her choice privileged the text—and its imagined power to disrupt and/or transform the prison—over the lives of real people. She justified this calculation by projecting blame onto the IRB for preventing her from having further contact with the *objects* of her study. This transfer of blame is unfortunately common. Barbara Tomlinson and George Lipsitz speak to the ways activist ideology gets distorted by neoliberal concerns in academic discourse:

> Part of the subjectivities of scholars has been produced by discourses that may seem "natural" to them, yet ultimately work against scholarly and political goals of antisubordination. Scholars who feel like victims of neoliberal hegemony may actually be working as its co-creators through the form and content of their academic arguments, their teaching, and their pursuit of recognition and reward. (7)

The IRB is not the sinister adversary of the virtuous scholar. As a scholar-teacher, I am responsible for my own consent to the structure of academic inquiry sanctioned by my institution. Nonetheless, the disconnection between the structures of study most readily available to me and my experiences in the prison classroom led me to seek out other ways of knowing and being that were more attendant to the humans I was working with, more intentionally humane. My search led me initially to ecosocial theory. In that body of scholarship, I found descriptions of human communities as *patches*, or ecosocial systems, where people interact with their social and material environments (Lemke 94). The idea of a patch challenges "the notion of 'the human individual' as a primary or privileged unit of analysis for any theory of human systems" (93).

At first, Lemke's work seemed to reflect what I observed in the writing classroom at New Folsom, attending as it does to the self-organizing, contingent nature of the interaction between human and nonhuman actors as they work to survive inside a "complex, hierarchically organized, developing and evolving ecosystem" (118). Prison bureaucracy does not make sense, but it nonetheless is hierarchically organized, with constantly evolving and devolving systems for managing incarcerated people. In this context, a writing community "changes constantly, driving itself toward new patterns of self-organizing by its very efforts to maintain the old ones" (130). That was true at New Folsom between 2003 and 2014, when job and program titles repeatedly changed and classes were taught by a patchwork of volunteers from the outside community and incarcerated teachers, all trying to hold on to the integrity of the program.

I found that ecosocial theory went a long way toward helping describe the organic, relational nature of humans in community (and in this case, humans in writing communities). In the context of composition, I could see how ecosocial theory provides a more relational Western frame for understanding the social and material location of community writing practices. It also echoes Tomlinson and Lipsitz's use of a relational, action-based metaphor in calling for more reflective, responsive, and responsible scholarship. For Tomlinson and Lipsitz, the metaphor for this type of work is *accompaniment,* and they describe two specific types of accompaniment actions: joining travelers on the road and joining in the making of music. They write that the metaphor of accompaniment allows scholars to "reinforce each other's dignity" while also recognizing the "inescapably and quintessentially social nature of both scholarship and citizenship" (10).

Variations on the themes of accompaniment and respect show up in composition scholarship as well. In their 2013 book, *Unsustainable: Re-imagining Community Literacy, Public Writing, Service-Learning and the University*, editors Jessica Restaino and Laurie JC Cella bring together scholarly voices who describe the complications of enacting respectful and reciprocal relations in university-sponsored projects. In her piece from the collection, Paula Mathieu suggests that there is still not enough research being done that really "explores how well community organizations are actually being served by university partnerships" ("After Tactics" 24). Likewise, in their contribution, Paul Feigenbaum, Sharayna Douglas, and Maria Lovett suggest that we should "strive to put people and relationships before institutional interests" and then go on to problematize the way institutional interests make the privileging of people and relationships unsustainable (34). Similarly, Lorelei Blackburn and Ellen Cushman suggest that relationships be studied as "central products" of community literacy work:

> In most of the community literacy scholarship that we have looked at, the product has been presumed to be of primary importance . . . the emphasis within the culture of community literacy is on the products that students create and on the products that community members need. And this makes perfect sense, because the products are one of the primary learning outcomes for outreach and engagement. However, because we argue that relationships are part of the product, we feel that a shift in focus is needed to enable consideration of not only how we produce end products/outcomes, but, more import, the relationships that we build along the way. (162)

Although Blackburn and Cushman's attention to the relationships that surround textual products is important, describing community relationships as "alternative products" showcases again the difficulty of moving away from an economics-based colonial discourse. Blackburn and Cushman's use of capitalistic language exemplifies the struggle of trying to ascribe and assess the value of community relationships in a way that both respects communities and benefits the scholar-teachers whose institutional allegiances require them to account, very often in economic terms, for their professional endeavors.

Despite its problematically capitalistic language, Blackburn and Cushman's piece highlights one of the persistent issues with the forays of writing scholars into the community: "Rhet/Comp scholars usually consider writing as the product of engagement initiatives. However, when we focus on writing as the product, then, after the writing is finished, no further interaction between the community, students, professors, or university is needed" (175). Blackburn and Cushman's observation specifically describes a key ethical issue with situating the university at the center of both the *what* and *for whom* of many of our research projects. The perpetuation of the university as a colonizing center whose doors close when what was needed has been taken will continue until the methodological frames explicitly require something different.

By moving away from the idea of "writing as the product of engagement," scholars can dispense with an overvaluing of individual textual artifacts. They can also stop relying on such texts as demonstrable proofs of the value and function of writing. However, moving away from text-extraction-as-proof presents its own set of ethical problems. Where individual writers do not enter the discourse via their own voices, for example, there is the distinct possibility of misrepresentation, appropriation, and/or entanglement with the countless other ethical concerns that are regularly taken up by the IRB. Dismantling the notion of the discrete, knowable, demonstrable text and setting all writing in an organic, relational context, all the while realizing that a problematic colonial sensibility is always at hand, can be a recipe for disaster. This is particularly true when those texts end up serving the scholar-teacher more than the scholar-teacher serves the community (as I imagine was the case with the scholar mentioned earlier who planned to publish despite the risk to the incarcerated people on whom her work was focused).

Sometimes a writer's word cannot hold together outside its moment in the way that we want it to. This is particularly true of words born in spaces like prisons, which are obscured from the public eye. Consider the following example. In the prison classrooms where I teach, group members will often exchange text. Sometimes a writer will connect emotionally with his audience, causing beautiful ruptures in the typical prison postures of distance and protective emotional closure. Words on the page form a type of local currency, a gift economy of sorts. And yet, I have found that the word-gifts that I have been given do not always hold their power as I would expect them to once outside the prison walls. When I have tried to share these word-gifts with friends outside the prison, almost everything is lost in the rhetorical distance between the classroom where the words were born and the space where I have tried to share them. Such moments of psychic disequilibrium have led me to look for methodologies that do not require or that significantly cut down on the need to wave around student papers (or more likely, read them in a solemn voice in front of small audiences at dimly lit coffee shops).

This disconnect between inside writer and outside audience reflects the *terministic screens* (to use Burke's term), or the rhetorical explanations and definitions, that encapsulate the US prison and make it almost impossible for people outside to engage in relaxed, open postures of listening to the words of incarcerated writers. It is less about the quality and power of the texts being generated by incarcerated writers than about the ideological atmosphere around the listener. (Here I am thinking of the very nice, suburban white woman who cuts my hair and likes to spend some of our time together talking about her favorite prison-themed shows on Netflix.) I share my experience observing the disconnect between inside writer and outside audience as a means of reaffirming our need to reconsider what a context-less text is really capable of doing. If a text cannot hold together and be used as proof in an academic study of the prison classroom, then we should probably seek other options for leveraging our positions inside the academy and supporting the work of incarcerated writers and teachers. The theoretical foundations of ethical attempts at leveraging our positions require more distance from coloniality than what Western methodologies afford. This is not to say we must wholly reject Western theory. As Margaret Kovach writes, Western theory still has its place and even shares some aspects with Indigenous methodologies in such spheres as "feminism, autoethnography, phenomenology, and narrative inquiry" that use story to build knowledge (96). She suggests that "we need to use all the very best available theoretical and methodological tools," but that we also need to "develop new approaches when these tools are inadequate" (91). A writing classroom functioning inside a purposefully dehumanizing institutional context is one example of a location where Western theory is inadequate.

### HOW IT IS: INDIGENOUS SCHOLARS ON RELATIONALITY

Because Indigenous theory deals directly with the reality of coloniality as a present-day (rather than historical) context, it provides an ideological locus separate from the coloniality of Western thought. This theoretical distance is particularly important in prison education work, where complicity with injustice is inescapable. Here, I share how the work of Indigenous scholars can be applied to the context of the prison classroom. To quote Todd, my intentions are to "reference Indigenous thinkers in a direct, contemporary and meaningful way . . . without filtering ideas through white intermediaries [and] by citing and quoting Indigenous thinkers directly, unambiguously and generously" (7). The work of Vine Deloria, V. F. Cordova, and Eber Hampton speaks directly to the call for decolonial theories. Furthermore, a host of composition scholars has contributed to the body of Indigenous theory in composition.[2] Rather than serving as teleological nodes on a linear progression of discipline-specific theory, these scholars ask us to reconsider what we think we see when we use our scholarly eye.

Looking to Indigenous scholars in the formation of decolonial theories is a purposeful choice to "learn from thinkers from our own hemisphere" (Villanueva, "On the Rhetoric" 659). Such a move begins to check "our easy and narrow reliance on Greek, Roman, European, and even European American thinkers" (Powell, "Down" 39). Disrupting the easy reliance on Western scholars also requires a disruption of Western epistemologies, so that as we are listening to scholars from this hemisphere we are also listening with and through the epistemologies that frame the knowledge such scholars share (Powell, "2012 CCCC"; Kovach). For example, many Indigenous scholars describe a nonlinear philosophy of being in the world that long precedes linear academic designs (see, for example, Cordova; Deloria, "Philosophy," *Spirit*; Hampton; Mihesuah and Wilson; Weber-Pillwax; and S. Wilson).

Vine Deloria explains that the Plains Indians "arranged their knowledge in a circular format—which is to say, there were no ultimate terms or constituents of their universe, only sets of relationships that sought to describe phenomena" (*Spirit* 48). A circular format for knowledge is distinctly different from a teleological one, and the implications of this way of understanding how knowledge works are profound. A theory of knowledge as an array of related units that inform and stabilize our conception of "here" is very different from a theory of knowledge as metaphorical building blocks that help us build up and away from "here" on some linear, future-oriented progression.

"The development of Western science was based on the idea that human beings could abstract themselves from the observational and experimental situation," writes Deloria. "They could then devise objective principles that would be applicable at any time or place in reasonably similar situations" (*Spirit* 64). In contrast, "tribal knowledge systematically mixes facts and experiences that Western science would separate by artificial categories" (67). Deloria describes this Western methodology of reductionism as the "tendency to divide, subdivide, and subdivide again in order to find the constituents of an entity or event" (129). This Western method works against a study of organic connections, leaving gaping blind spots in our theoretical understanding of the what, why, and how of composition.

Anne Waters notes that the claim of an always already relationality in Indigenous thought does not "romanticize," but rather articulates, "a theory of knowing through synthetic processes" (xviii). Interconnectedness in Indigenous thought, Waters adds, takes the form of "we," not "I." Indeed, the concept of a "we" runs throughout the essays in Water's edited collection. Similarly, Cordova calls for paying close attention to what it means to be human in the world. Working to answer this question, she argues, helps us understand the world and our responsibility to make it—to act as co-creators. In the foreword to *How It Is: The Native American Philosophy of V. F. Cordova*, Linda Hogan summarizes Cordova's work as suggesting that "[w]e are co-creators in the universe, the world, within all the rest, all fluid, shifting movement, and without the emphasis on measurement. The world is there in its entirety, not in segments" (xi).

This notion of seeing ourselves as co-creators presumes an understanding that we are in relationship with everything around us—even when we are operating within the most totalizing of institutions. According to Cordova, "the Native American concept of the relatedness of all beings" is a foundational concept "for other ideas and practices" (67). Relationality forms a key part of the epistemological bedrock underpinning the critique of observable, measurable, individual persons. It also pushes against practices that work to separate, categorize, and isolate, encouraging instead a deep, holistic understanding of our relationships and the ways that we use language in the ongoing processes of co-creation of which we are always already a part, even and maybe especially within institutions.

Speaking to the inadequacy of a Western dismissal of the relatedness of things, Eber Hampton writes frankly:

> Emotionless, passionless, abstract, intellectual, academic research is a goddamn lie, it does not exist. It is a lie to ourselves and a lie to other people. Humans—feeling, living, breathing, thinking humans—do research. When we try to cut ourselves off at the neck and pretend an objectivity that does not exist

in the human world, we become dangerous, to ourselves first, and then to people around us. (52)

Here Hampton points out a real danger in the pretense of objectivity, shifting the whole conversation about modernity and coloniality in academic inquiry to an urgently political space. And it is on urgently political ground that prison writing programs currently function. If Hampton is right that we cannot cut ourselves off at the neck, and if Cordova more closely describes the reality in which scholar-teachers function, then we will have to reconsider what we think we see when we use our scholarly eye to look in on the prison classroom.

One option for learning to look again is purposeful listening without the intent to master. Judy Atkinson describes this as "[a] deep listening and hearing with more than the ears" (qtd. in S. Wilson 59). Deep listening, she suggests, is predicated on important relational work. In fact, listening is the sixth item in her list of guiding principles for conducting research with aboriginal people, farther down the page from the initial, explicit approval of both the study and the methods by the community being studied. Speaking here is understood as a dialectic between community members, and a diversity of community voices is privileged over individual writers or texts. My first research project at New Folsom missed that mark by a mile.

Indigenous methodologies can richly inform the construction of research projects that study the living, breathing humans who make up prison writing communities. In particular, Shawn Wilson's construction of an Indigenous methodology raises essential questions about *relationality* and *relational accountability* that can be applied to the study of prison writing programs, inform academic inquiry at its core, and challenge the central questions of what counts as research, how it is collected, who owns it, and how it is evaluated and distributed. Both Wilson and Smith make clear that their primary intended audiences are Indigenous scholars who already understand and speak from positions informed by Indigenous ideologies. They suggest employing academic methodologies rooted in cultural practices that are already familiar to Indigenous scholars.

Although I do not claim personal knowledge of these cultural practices, I do see how the contributions of both of these authors speak to, and resonate with, the friction inherent in applying traditional models of academic inquiry in places like prison.

In *Research Is Ceremony*, Wilson threads story and citation in the development of an Indigenous methodology for academic research, writing that "research is about unanswered questions, but also reveals our unquestioned answers" (6). His text is a response to the "unquestioned answers" of the Western research model, which has a long global history of disrespect and damage. Wilson calls for *respect, responsibility*, and *reciprocity* in academic research and suggests that these three tenets-in-action demand a deeply reflective understanding of the research process. He offers a circular paradigm for thinking about how the different aspects of a research project function in relation to each other, raising important questions all researchers should work to answer about what is real, how we know it to be so, and how to ethically gather and use information (34).

Wilson explains that relationships do not merely structure reality, but rather *are* reality, and should therefore be the cornerstone of any research project. He goes on to suggest that research topics, data collection methods, data analysis protocols, and presentations of data should all be informed by an attention to the "shared aspects of relationality and relational accountability" (7). Wilson suggests that "research is a ceremony" whose purpose is the strengthening of relationships and/or the bridging of distance (11). I appreciate Wilson's rhetorical move to eschew a discourse of salvation by development. For Wilson, the first purpose of research is the strengthening of existing relationships. The second purpose—the bridging of a distance—does the same subtle yet rhetorically significant work of suggesting a coming together of known things. Even though the language suggests movement, it is movement *between* and *toward*, not *away from*, the center.

Research as a means to relationship and connection is distinctly different than research as a means to measurable knowledge, which is the dominant view in academia. Smith suggests that where knowledge of the world is "reduced to issues of measurement, the focus of understanding becomes more concerned with procedural problems," which call for the development of "operational definitions of phenomena which are reliable and valid" (44). And paying close attention to concepts like reliability, validity, procedural problems, and operational definitions has led to the development of a discourse that obscures and openly discourages the recognition of relationality. My termination notice from the IRB is a good example of such discourse: It replaces my study title with a five-digit number and the generic appellation "human subject project." Jackson and Williams are labeled "human research participants" with whom "data collection and participant recruitment" has been "suspended."

I do not want to confuse a discussion of the limits of the discourse of Western research with a broad and sloppy antiscientism or step into the attack/counterattack that Downes and Rock describe between "charges of 'positivism'" and "obscurity or self-indulgence" (69). Like Mignolo, I see that decolonizing knowledge is not a rejection of "Western epistemic contributions to the world" but rather a loosening of the chains that link the acquisition of knowledge and "imperial designs" (82) so that other ways of knowing might be evoked. Looking for decolonial options is a purposeful legitimizing of "ways of knowing and sensing (feeling) that do not conform to the epistemology and aesthesis of the zero point"—ways of knowing that have otherwise been reinscribed as "myth, legend, folklore, local knowledge, and the like" (80). There is a place in the academy for a discourse of reliability, validity, procedure, and operations. And, of course, studies of living, breathing people should be clear, well-organized, and ethically accountable. But what is apparent in the way Western research discourse is often employed in the study of humans is a lingering colonial ideology that privileges quantifiable knowledge over holistic consideration that accounts for the relationships between the animate and inanimate aspects of any context.

## HOW PRISON SPACES CONSTRAIN RELATIONALITY

Within the context of the prison classroom there are no isolatable binaries—all animate and inanimate actors are related and implicated. Viewing the prison classroom through the prism of relationality requires that we consider the degree to which prison spaces constrain the relational possibilities of incarcerated people. This became clear to me when I taught in the mental health unit at New Folsom and experienced firsthand the powerful role that walls, tables, and chairs play in the success or failure of a class.[3] The room in the mental health unit had five round, immovable, stainless steel tables lining its perimeter with round, stainless steel stools bolted to the floor around each. A large picture window faced the corridor where a group of custody staff observed the class. There was no daylight or way to tell time. The concrete floor and walls, painted peachy-grey, produced a loud echo that made reading aloud nearly impossible. It was difficult to run a class in such an austere space. The participants were not combative, but I felt that I was not able to establish much connection, either between myself and the participants or among the class members.

Between my second and third visits, Carlson secured permission for the class to move to an unused staff meeting room. Though this new space still did not have outside light, it was free of the maddening echo of the previous classroom. Furthermore, the only window through which custody staff would observe was an eight-inch slit of glass in the door. The tables were moveable (they had been arranged in a U shape) and the chairs were padded. I took my seat at one end of the U and watched as class members entered the room for the first time. The effect of the new space on their body language was immediate. Students began to talk to each other and to me, and our session was noticeably more energetic than those in the other room had been.

Midway through the two-hour class, an officer came in and announced that the room was needed for staff purposes. We packed up and moved back to the original classroom space. The transition back to the constraints of stainless steel and echo drained the energy from the group despite my best efforts to mediate the change in the material environment. Being forced to move rooms mid-class was a really helpful lesson. In the juxtaposition of spaces it became totally clear how deeply everything is related—that there are direct connections even between the words that might be born in class and the type of chairs writers sit in.

Not only do teachers have to attend to how the material environment affects the quality of work and interaction therein, they are also responsible for the ways that their actions do or do not preserve and enhance the space itself. In the context of the highly contingent prison classroom, the relationship between the teacher and the material space is equally important to any of the human relationships that happen therein. The classroom space is a significant part of what fosters rich relationships between incarcerated writers, and between incarcerated writers and teachers. This is especially important in places like prison where the rules regarding overfamiliarity set up a binary between a privileging of human relationships and a sustaining of the spaces where deep human relationships come to be.

## RELATIONALITY AND (OVER)FAMILIARITY
### IN THE CARCERAL SPACE

One day, a few years into my teaching practice at New Folsom, I received an email from Carol Hinds, the mother of an AIC student. I immediately panicked and reported the incident, fully aware that contact with family members of incarcerated students was in contravention of prison rules against "overfamiliarity."[4] I knew of a few teachers who had forgotten or disregarded this imperative and lost their teaching posts because of it, and I had no intention of testing the limits. As it turns out, Hinds was a member of the Inmate Family Council, an oversight committee that met regularly with the warden. Because she had an official role at New Folsom and had also built her own relationship with the prison administration, our professional contact was sanctioned.

Since that first email, Hinds has been an invited speaker at the university twice and we have also presented together at multiple national conferences. (I have noticed that when Carol speaks at such conferences, attendees slip her notes, or whisper to her in the hall, or find her at the airport to share their own stories of loved ones caught up in the system.) But before she sent me that email,

Photo by Peter Merts.

she existed to me only in the sharp and powerful prose of her son, no more real in my mind than my favorite characters in literature. In reality she was an office manager of a medical practice, a mother whose only son was in prison, and a force of immense good and strategic advocacy in the lives of many incarcerated people. When she emailed me, I was forced to expand my understanding of the relational reality of the prison classroom to include her. And once I made space for Carol, I began to see that the incarcerated writers I knew at New Folsom had not been quite erased in the ways that the scholarship was suggesting.

I very often hear prison scholar-teachers complaining—for good reason—about the cruel, seemingly arbitrary, and decidedly inhuman bureaucracy of the carceral state. Sometimes teachers are turned away at the gate for a clothing violation despite having worn the same shirt inside six times before. Some programs are only allowed to use golf pencils. Others do not allow writers to keep their writing at the end of class. The stories are endless and reflect the fatiguing nature of work inside. So the idea that a warden would allow a mom and a university professor to communicate directly and build a professional relationship is unusual but not outside the realm of possibility where the relational threads—in this case, between a mother with an incarcerated son and the warden, and between the AIC and the prison—have been well tended. Since our first contact, both Carol and I have respected the institutional rules that prohibit overfamiliarity. And although that respect for the rules has sometimes slowed down or made our communications more cumbersome, the work we have been able to do together has been worth the fatigue. Carlson similarly attributes both his longevity inside, and his rich history of orchestrating collaborative projects between incarcerated artists and the outside community, to his close attention to such rules. This attention has built a workable trust between AIC and the institution. As discussed, such a trust has allowed the program to persist in evolving form through the sweeping budgetary cuts that wiped out every other program of its kind in the state.

### ACCOUNTABLE RELATIONSHIPS THAT COUNTER THE COLONIAL IMPULSE TO DEHUMANIZE

Cultivating relationality in the prison classroom includes paying attention to the relationships between teachers, students, and the spaces in which they meet. It also requires an attention to the relationship between teachers and custody staff, as well as teachers and prison administrators. To the extent that any of these relational threads are neglected or overtaxed, the relational circle loses its integral form. But making sense of our relationships, and accounting honestly for the ways that those relationships rub and sometimes blister in contact with other relationships is fraught, if not impossible.

Wilson's framework for relational accountability offers an ideological litmus of sorts for assessing relationality in academic inquiry, particularly the fundamental power structures between researcher and researched. Relational accountability informs the ethical parameters of research activity, particularly in the asking of questions about what scholars do to gain knowledge and what/how that knowledge is used (S. Wilson 7). Relational accountability also frames questions of methodology, or how we go about finding out more about the realities that spark academic inquiry.

However, in the tangled mess of dehumanizing institutional rules and the horrors of everyday life in prison, it is sometimes difficult for scholar-teachers to make sense of what relational accountability might look like. To be specific, it can be hard to observe the dehumanizing conditions of prison without wanting to "do something" that "saves" incarcerated writers from the deprivation and chaos of living behind bars. Yet as I previously discussed and as Jackson and Williams reminded me often, the role of "missionary" that many prison scholar-teachers slip into is fundamentally unhelpful and a serious breach of relational accountability in that it reifies unequal power relations between outside teachers or researchers and incarcerated writers. Any attempt to rescue, heal, or fix ultimately ascribes to those on the outside a power that is not theirs and reinvigorates the colonial rhetoric of salvation by development. Although I worked to avoid the trap of imagining that I was "saving" incarcerated writers, I have come to see a handful of ways I inadvertently dehumanized the writers with whom I worked, both by making assumptions about their ability to relate to me and by taking some of their writing choices personally.

Before I began teaching at the prison, I knew I needed to establish my ethos as a writer by bringing some of my own work to read. Because the only personal writing I was doing at that time was about parenting young children, I was tempted to fabricate or liberally stretch my own stories to an unrecognizable place that I imagined would make me more relatable to a group of incarcerated men between the ages of eighteen and sixty-five.

In the tension between what I could offer and the false self I was tempted to construct were stereotypes about prison, gender, race, fatherhood, and who knows what else. My wondering about whether or not my writing would connect with an incarcerated audience presumed a very low opinion—and I would say even subscribed a subhuman status—to the group of writers with whom I would be meeting. Despite every intention to the contrary, the fabrications I was considering implicitly devalued the humanness in the writers I planned to work with by assuming they would not be able to connect with the humanness I had written into my own texts—a dangerous and damaging assumption.

In the end, I did bring the work that I had and shared it as honestly as I could. My choice to be myself, as unrelatable as I imagined I might be, was a good one. As it turned out, my stories about parenting small children were a welcome reprieve for writers used to reading about prison-related themes. I had not considered that talking about my kids would be interpreted as a sign of respect, but as many of the writers in the class pointed out, most people who come to the prison chose not to share much about their life outside. Many times that impulse is a response to prison rules about overfamiliarity. Other times it is a conscious, personal choice. Either way, the writing classroom provides a fruitful, even if fraught, opening for personal expression. And that opening allowed me to demonstrate relational accountability through an appropriately professional sharing from my own life through stories of motherhood.

Another example of the dehumanizing impulse at work concerns my reaction to a writer who I felt disrespected the group by consistently bringing fiction to a class about nonfiction narrative. In talking with Williams about my frustration, I came to see that I was personalizing this writer's choice not to write from the details of his own life—details he may have had good reason to leave buried. Williams shared with me a similar frustration early in his teaching experience and said he came to realize that relational accountability in the classroom space had to balance a respect for assigned tasks with a deep and welcoming patience.

The writer in question did eventually write from his own experience, and when he did a part of me was sorry for having taken his use of fiction so personally. In retrospect, I could see that he was using fiction as a bridge to nonfiction: he needed time—years—to weigh the real consequences of opening his life up both to himself and to his classmates. This story reminds me that where I have allowed feelings of personal affront, I have privileged my own plans and timelines for the classroom over a relational accountability to the writers within it. Reflecting on our assumptions and how they might conflict with our intentions is a crucial practice for educators who seek relationality in all contexts, but especially in prisons.

Writing about the destructive outcome of white educators' hyper-focus on the education of First Nations kids, Hampton makes the following observation: "[W]hen I start asking *why* about somebody else's behavior, I should ask *why* about my own" (50). Hampton's critique of the well-intentioned white educator suggests several questions on which all prison scholar-teachers might do well to reflect: Why am I volunteering at the prison? Is it to change people's lives? To see them become more political? To notch my teaching belt with some novel experience? Are my motives altruistic? And if they are, are the questions I am asking arising from a deep listening to the community? Summarizing Cora Weber-Pillwax, Shawn Wilson lists additional questions on which scholar-teachers might reflect before they burden a community with their research project:

- How do my methods help to build respectful relationships between the topic I am studying and myself as researcher (on multiple levels)?
- How do my methods help to build respectful relationships between myself and the other research participants?
- How can I relate respectfully to the other participants involved in this research so that together we can form a stronger relationship with the idea that we will share?
- What is my role as researcher in this relationship, and what are my responsibilities?
- Am I being responsible in fulfilling my role and obligations to the other participants, to the topic, and to all of my relations?
- What I am contributing or giving back to the relationship? Is the sharing, growth, and learning that is taking place reciprocal? (S. Wilson 77)

These questions get to the heart of the matter—to the motivations and memories that Eber Hampton asks researchers to uncover before they begin their research.

## A FIVE-PART INTERPRETIVE FRAMEWORK FOR
## TEACHING AND RESEARCH IN PRISONS

In *Indigenous Methodologies*, Margaret Kovach describes how she "utilized a methodology based upon an Indigenous research framework centered on Plains Cree knowledge." Kovach's application of those principles brought her to an Indigenous research (conceptual) framework with six interrelated characteristics: "(a) tribal epistemology, (b) decolonizing and ethical aim, (c) researcher preparation involving cultural protocols, (d) research preparation involving standard research design, (e) making meaning of knowledge gathered, and (f) giving back" (45). As a non-Indigenous scholar, I cannot (and would not) claim that my teaching and research practices are rooted in tribal epistemology. Yet despite my position as an outsider with limited knowledge, I can see that Kovach's conceptual framework provides some clear guidelines and guardrails for researchers and sponsors undertaking decolonial projects in the prison context.

I have attempted to construct an interpretive methodological framework based on, and aligned as closely as possible with, Kovach's model, but with an audience of non-Indigenous prison program researchers and sponsors in mind. I use the word *community* twice in the model because of its rhetorical power and currency in the prison context. I have also merged the areas of knowledge-gathering and meaning-making to highlight for prison scholar-teachers the reality that making-meaning of any knowledge gathered in a prison requires the involvement of incarcerated people. My modified version of Kovach's model asks scholars to look again at what they see with their scholarly eye and to privilege an epistemological position that acknowledges that relationships already are at the root of any knowledge-making process.

As an example of the process of looking again at what is already there, a relational ontology is fairly easy to identify in the context of prison work once it is pointed out. Absolutely no one enters a prison classroom without an official relationship to the prison apparatus and the requisite papers that authorize admission. Likewise, the relational web incarcerated people navigate (often including gang affiliation) is the basis for almost all of the sanctioned activities, implicit rules, and underground goings-on of daily life behind bars. It makes perfect sense, then, that any methodology for such a place would benefit from a relational ontology. Furthermore, almost anyone teaching in the prison will concede that the establishment of respectful relationships between teachers and incarcerated students must precede any knowledge-making work. And because unrelenting dehumanization of life in prison makes many incarcerated students particularly sensitive to issues of respect, a methodology aligned with an Indigenous understanding of relationality and respect holds a lot of promise.

With all of that said, Cordova points out that Indigenous philosophy has often been misinterpreted through the claim that a "common set of beliefs" exists which "leads the philosopher astray in picking and choosing bits and pieces from the alien culture to satisfy the longing for a common theme" (59). Likewise, historically, "within an Indigenous research context, the result has been an attempt to weld Indigenous methods to existing bodies of Western knowledge, resulting in confused efforts and methodological floundering" (Kovach 36). In what follows, I have attempted to listen (as closely as I am able) with and through the epistemologies that inform ways of knowing distinct from Western schools of thought. I hope that I have eschewed the historical welding or ornamentation that Cordova and Kovach warn against.

Each of the five elements in my interpretation of Kovach's framework should be understood as part of an interconnected whole. When taken together, these elements ask scholar-teachers working in the prison to consider the relationships between their teaching and/or research; the colonial legacies that inspired and sustain prison education; their personal motivations; the cultural assets and articulated needs of incarcerated students; and the connections incarcerated students have to communities outside the prison. The five elements of my modified version (Plemons, "Beyond" 85–86) of Kovach's model are as follows:

1. **Decolonial Intention and Ethic:** Researchers are committed to examining how both individuals and groups have been affected by and complicit in colonial legacies. Furthermore, they are committed to asking questions that challenge the Western knowledge systems that define what is real and how we know it to be such (Haas, "Toward").

2. **Researcher Preparation:** Researchers are committed to exploring their own relationships to the research or project, finding and making sense of the memories and stories that inform their motivation for the work (Hampton).

3. **Community Accountability:** The research project responds to the articulated needs and/or desires of the community, evolves in response to community feedback, and is terminated when or if the community decides that the project is at odds with its health and sovereignty (S. Wilson).

4. **Reciprocity/Community Benefit:** The research project respects participants as already valuable members of their respective communities and directly works to support community members in those existing roles. Benefits to the community, made primarily by the community members themselves, are part of the clearly articulated outcomes of the research project (S. Wilson).

5. **Knowledge Gathering/Meaning-Making:** The types of knowledge gathered though the project and the meanings that are constructed about that knowledge privilege the community over the individual as the unit of analysis, balances a need for data with a respect for participants' desire to protect sacred and/or private knowledge, and directly includes the community in the process of meaning-making and subsequent distribution of knowledge (Kovach).

In Chapter 4, I describe two projects at New Folsom that make use of this interpretive framework of Kovach's work.

# WRITERS AND TEACHERS, PART 4

**Tommy**

I walked by him every day for two weeks without so much as a chin dip. This stranger in a wheelchair with his swollen legs and bloated torso, the heavy face and piercing blue eyes. He was dying and everybody knew it. But he had money and generosity so they stayed close. I walked by and walked by not needing another friend and especially not one so close to the grave. What was the point? Still, our paths eventually crossed with an obligatory handshake, tight lipped smile and "alright now"-type flat affirmation usually reserved for insecure/dominant male greetings. He had a firm, if fleshy handshake and the sort of ill-at-ease confidence I would come to recognize in terminal cases. I stood around with the herd for awhile exchanging petty banter and trying my best not to interact with him directly. Something in every one of his very few movements spoke of frustration and anger. He sat in that wheelchair with his puffy hands folded over a distended stomach doing all he could to give the impression of control; but he was a horse trapped in a burning barn with nowhere to go, nothing to do but make a valiant effort at dignity kept. Never once did I imagine what he thought of me. Over the months that followed circumstances thrust us together, finding ourselves in the same places at the same time every other night, discovering a green branch bond, a regulated trust. This wasn't easy, as neither of us was blind to the other's faults; the biggest being our own ways of judging people too hard, too quick. Interestingly, the closer we became the more others dropped away. All relationships require maintenance—his required an added physical/emotional sort most people were not willing to undertake. As usually happens, I would find myself the most responsible, silently volunteering to stay later, push him to the med nurse and then back home for the night. I didn't realize at the time it was in these brief moments our most enduring bonds would be formed. Away from the groups we changed, softened, relaxed and showed vulnerability. His embarrassment would bloom knowing I saw the handfuls of meds and cup after cup of thick, syrupy liquid he would try to hold down. I learned to stay the course during minor traumas, and in so doing, was rewarded with his trust above all: don't look away from the sores when he stands up—you might not see, and therefore stop, the fall; do look away when he vomits his medication into the toilet, into the bucket he keeps on the back of his wheelchair, onto the floor in front of everyone; always volunteer to clean the vomit and *always* without drama or disgust, so he keeps his dignity, so you can pick through it to find which meds stayed and which ones left; know when to call for a nurse *now*; but know when to clean his face first. Three years ticked by, neither of us paying enough attention to notice the earth slowing down. I finally met Tommy, my friend, and he finally knew me. But he was dying and everybody knew it.

—Adam Hinds

## The Fist Pump

I was granted a resentencing hearing and had gotten sent back to Orange County Superior Court and then denied without explanation. While on my bus ride back up North here to New Folsom, I began to envision myself on the other side of the tinted window bus, waving at the faceless prisoners like a tortured fanatic for the struggles beyond the common.

Along the ride, I had seen two cars among the thousands that waved ever-so-kindly. One of them opened the sunroof and fist-pumped the air. At that immediate moment, as I instinctively gawked around the bus to see if anyone saw or even cared about the sighting of the royal fist pump I just witnessed, I noticed that they were not even looking in that direction. Not one man was looking. Only me? Only me!! That fist pump was for Ronnie! This felt so good—like he was giving money to the homeless, or in my case, hope to the hopeless, without the expectation of a "Thank You." It felt like he had been in prison before or maybe had family in prison himself. But mostly, it felt as if he directly knew of my resentencing denial and sent me this message of hope.

It wasn't a straight ride back up North, as CDCR will always tend to lay over inmates going on statewide transfers. So, our bus happened to be in North Kern, and though it was only for one night, my mind had picked fruit from the surrounding hearts. So much fruit, in fact, that it deserved this mention. The evening of the lay-over, before the second day of the trip up North, the Housing Assignment Officer had placed me in a cell with a Korean fellow that used to run with the Black population on his prior prison terms, but due to the total of two strikes on his record, he needed to avoid further conflict. So, in his theory, running with the Asian population would propose a lesser risk of drama.

First off, let me note that he took psych medication and was a little different than the average, attentive, and conscious human being, as he did lack certain social skills that strained fluid communication. Nevertheless, a human in need is a human indeed, and although it was difficult at times, I found a way to keep the conversation flowing for three steady hours before I went to bed.

I'm glad I did stay up and relay my genuine concern for his habitual nature of fighting, recklessness, and need of approval or acceptance from others at the cost of his ethical values.

I knew he had a kind heart that would lose control or explode if he were hurt or neglected, and I could see the raw pain as he took his PM medication after dinner to forget the confusion that became his life of violence, and though he was 32, I still somehow caught a glimpse of my reflected self ten years ago when I was just as frustrated at the world. Suddenly, then, I began to see parts of myself in that present self that I still needed to fix.

I remind myself each day that in order to do this, I must help others through my experiences, so maybe they can see that there is always another option to express their abilities and value. And, in the case of my Korean buddy, options without violence and dependency on prescription medication.

In gratitude to these scattered thoughts, I am blessed to have gained a smidgeon of wisdom in the selfless deeds I've acted upon. I guess in life there truly is intention and purpose in all we say and do. And though we don't see it just yet, there is a common purpose we haven't yet realized. Something above the wedding vows and honeymoons. Above the nice house and family vacations. Above looking forward to the past we still can't see in our rear view.

Prison life. The body goes about its day and weak hearts find a place to stray. Yet we can't deny that we are connected, that you feel my presence while unwrapping this lettered present. We can only fist pump the air to the unknown watcher, looking for hope as I once did.

—Hung-Linh "Ronnie" Hoang

## Getting Healthy

He looks so young that it is hard for me to imagine he has a son in high school. His existence in this windowless room infantilizes, messes with my ideas of time, age, adulthood. Tattoos creep up his neck and onto the side of his face. He sometimes comes to the writing group, accruing hours of federally mandated recreational therapy for those with pronounced mental illness. He has been coming to class on and off for a few years. When he comes to class we swap stories—I talk about kids and school, he talks about coming up through foster care, the nice folks he really wanted to please but just couldn't at the horse ranch, and deciding which fights to pick in prison.

He comes in today with a four-inch garden lizard clinging to his crisp white tee shirt. He sits in his regular seat to my left—close to the teacher, but not too close. The lizard explores the tabletop, ventures onto my stack of papers, blinks, breathes, turns around. While the group discusses synecdoche, he gently scratches under the lizard's jaw with the tip of his ballpoint pen. He leaves early, again.

The guy next to him is handsome, well spoken, a spoken word artist with dreads. He makes thoughtful comments, reads some of his work to start the class. With twenty minutes remaining, a clinician in a stab vest comes in with a clipboard, sits down next to him. I don't know what to do with her presence; she does not introduce herself, does not volunteer to read aloud.

With five minutes left she gets up without saying anything. The man with dreads turns to her, "Make sure to write something negative about me," he says. "Say that I was uncooperative, a nuisance. Otherwise they plan to send me back to the Mainline."

She smiles, jests—"I'll say you spit at me."

He smiles back, nods his head.

I collect my papers with my head down, a red-hot rope running up my spine.

—Anna Plemons

# 4

## Opportunities and Options: Relationality at New Folsom

It is difficult to explain that the mundane is actually the sacred.
—V. F. Cordova, *How It Is*

IN WRITING THIS BOOK, I HAVE worried that readers may be tempted to throw the proverbial baby out with the bathwater—that is, to stop working in places like prisons where our complicity in the lives of writers and our defaulting to the structures of coloniality implicate us in the worst kinds of injustices. I also worry that the contribution I have tried to make to the conversation about decoloniality and methodological options will be dismissed as not close enough to a Western center to be of consequence. In short, I am equally worried about those who might run off and do something rash and those who will do nothing at all.

Clearly the work of overcoming a sedimented coloniality in the field of composition remains unfinished. And in the spirit of things unfinished, this chapter eschews any definitive conclusion. As I've emphasized throughout this book, prison writing programs, like most community writing programs, are contingent, complicated, and decidedly local. Therefore, I do not propose a one-size-fits-all solution to the concerns raised here. I do, however, suggest that we look closely at the influence of colonial ideologies on our epistemology and on the structures of study to which we consent. By embracing an ontology of relationality, prison scholar-teachers can directly challenge a rhetoric of erasure that misrepresents the level of connection and commitment many incarcerated students still have to communities outside the prison, as well as the overuse of individual narratives of transformation that misrepresent the relational complexity of any one person's story. They can also challenge deficit ideologies that are incapable of accounting for the ways that incarcerated students continue to operate as community and cultural assets both inside and outside the prison.

Although the projects discussed in this chapter have proven rewarding for participants, there is no grand victory story to tell here. These projects should be understood as small, local attempts at work done in the spirit of decoloniality. I hope these projects help make the case for why we need a wider array of methodological and assessment options, but they do not presume to singlehandedly solve the problem of mass incarceration or dismantle the ideological foundation on which it rests. As Kovach has aptly noted, "waking up to a new fully decolonized day would be wonderful if unlikely. The process is more fluid and modestly incremental with 'strategic concessions' all over the place, but we are making headway. After all, co-dependency is one wicked little web from which to disentangle" (129). It is with that wicked web in mind that I proceed with a collection of options for relational work evidenced in the life of Arts in Corrections past and present.

## HISTORICAL SNAPSHOTS OF RELATIONALITY IN ARTS IN CORRECTIONS

While not every project associated with the AIC program can be described as having been relational or decolonial, I review here two projects where the creators made a conscious effort to respect the needs of the overlapping communities involved: The ArtsWork project and the Swedish documentary *At Night I Fly* (Wenzer).

### ArtsWork

Not long after the inception of the AIC program, incarcerated artists and AIC faculty began imagining and enacting collaborative projects with communities inside and outside the prison. In many cases, the impetus for the projects was an expressed interest on the part of incarcerated artists to participate in meaningful ways with the arts community outside the prison. These organic, individual projects eventually led, in the mid-1980s, to the establishment of ArtsWork, "an innovative statewide prison-based public art program" (Cleveland, *Art*). Cleveland notes that "as a result, members of more than 100 communities throughout the state have experienced prisons and the people who live and work in them as highly visible community contributors." Cleveland offers the following examples of ArtsWork projects:

- "Inmate artists, organized as a permanent mural crew at the California Institution for Women, prepared backdrop scenery for a theatrical production by the Exceptional Children's Foundation, a Los Angeles-based program for children with developmental disabilities."
- As discussed in this book as well, an inmate production of Samuel Beckett's *Waiting for Godot* was performed at San Quentin Prison and proceeds benefited Bay Area victims' rights organizations.
- "The combined efforts of muralists from the California Institution for Men and the California Institution for Women produced a series of permanent murals for the senior center at Angeles Plaza in downtown Los Angeles."
- "A joint community mural project instituted at the California Training Facility at Soledad produced 10 outdoor murals for the cities of Oceanside, Monterey, and Gonzales." (*Art* 60–61)

I think it is significant that many ArtsWork projects focused on supporting children and the elderly. Based on my own experience teaching inside, I imagine that cross-generational connections were made in response to the participating artists' expressed interests.

In *By Heart*, Spoon Jackson writes extensively about his experiences performing in *Godot*, highlighting how the production literally opened up San Quentin to folks who would not have had interest or access otherwise:

During the later stages of rehearsal, nearly every day someone from Beckett's world showed up to give advice and to see how the play progressed. Theater groups from San Francisco and elsewhere in the Bay Area stopped by; drama students from Stanford, Cal, and San Francisco State came in. Theater folk and directors from France, Sweden, and Austria came by. Some Swedish royalty also visited. Alice Smith, from San Francisco's American Conservatory Theater, volunteered as our stage manager and acting coach. (Tannenbaum and Jackson 104)

At one point during the lead-up to *Godot*, the director, Jan Jönson, gave Samuel Beckett a chapbook of Jackson's poems. Jackson writes about how significant it was for him to know that Beckett had read his work (105). Both the ArtsWork mural projects and the *Godot* production reflect relationality in the details of the relationships that formed through them and in small yet significant gestures of connection like Jönson's connecting of Jackson and Beckett. It is also represented in the longitudinal look at how relationships were sustained once the projects ended. As evidenced by their joint memoir, Jackson and Judith Tannenbaum, the poetry teacher who first encouraged Jackson to audition, are still in contact. Jönson has also returned to visit Jackson in prison, as has his daughter.

### At Night I Fly

Before the US premiere of *At Night I Fly* at the Museum of Modern Art in New York City, filmmaker Michel Wenzer returned to New Folsom to watch the film with AIC participants. Although there was no way for incarcerated participants to directly influence and shape the film editing process and the project does not adhere to a relational methodology, Wenzer's return to the prison was a show of respect and a gesture without precedent in the history of the AIC.

After the showing at New Folsom, Wenzer met with a few of the men who featured prominently in the film to discuss their reaction. It was an emotional encounter. One participant in the debriefing pointed out that other film crews, including one from National Geographic, had come to the prison but absolutely no one had ever come back. It was important to Wenzer that the first people in the United States to see the film be the incarcerated men who read their poems before the cameras. And his choice to come back after the completion of the film exemplifies what community literacy scholars like Blackburn and Cushman are aiming for: relationships that outlive projects.

## RELATIONALITY AND THE REINSTATEMENT OF ARTS IN CORRECTIONS

As mentioned earlier in this book, the AIC program officially ended in 2003. The remaining artist facilitators around the state who had taken posts in the education program were given pink slips in 2009. Jim Carlson then moved to Mental Health Services and starting using two words to describe art programs that he had spent all of his AIC years disavowing: *therapy* and *recreation*. He made these two significant rhetorical concessions strategically. Because the federal mandate for mental health services requires people receiving mental health supervision to receive both therapy and recreation, the new iteration of AIC received nominal funds from Mental Health Services cobbled together from the Inmate Welfare Fund and private donations. Reshaping AIC so that it fit inside a rhetoric of mental health bought the new AIC some crucial time while the political dust of the old program's demise settled.

Meanwhile, Carlson championed the AIC program in both political and public circles, appearing before a state senate committee on the arts, for example, and securing an audience with the California Inspector General three times (twice as a public commenter and once as an invited speaker on the agenda). He has also traveled, mostly at his own expense, to *At Night I Fly* screenings in Connecticut, New York, California, and Canada, conducting question-and-answer sessions following the screenings. Additionally, since 2003, he and his wife have housed and fed most of the volunteers he has brought to the prison as well as organized house concerts for the musicians to offset the personal expenses they accrue as volunteers. For Carlson and others, the work of keeping AIC alive has been exhausting and personal. Their actions typify Paula Mathieu's description of community work:

> I now realize how hard, and perhaps inevitably unsustainable, tactical, hopeful community work can be. Committing

oneself to starting a project also means inevitably facing an ending, sometimes a painful one. Tactical work requires—or at least signs us up for—a continual act of reinvention, of starting from scratch, going back to square one and having the courage to face the possibility of work not happening, but hoping and working so it will. And sometimes things come full circle. ("After Tactics" 18)

In 2012 a pilot of the remixed AIC program was conducted at San Quentin, New Folsom, Salinas Valley State Prison, and Soledad. The September 15, 2013, Biannual Report of the California Rehabilitation Oversight Board (C-ROB), chaired by the California Inspector General, strongly suggested that AIC be (re)instituted at a statewide level: "The board reviewed the Arts in Corrections pilot program and is pleased with the initial results. The department should continue working toward developing a dedicated Arts in Corrections program, to be administered statewide." C-ROB recommended that the State of California allocate $1.214 million over two years to develop AIC programs at nine institutions (California Rehabilitation Oversight Board 28). The C-ROB report also detailed collaboration between the California Arts Council (CAC), California Lawyers for the Arts (CLA), and the William James Association, with CLA bringing in grant monies from the California Arts Council, National Endowment for the Arts, and the Andy Warhol, Wallace Alexander Gerbode, and San Francisco Foundations. In 2015, additional monies were set aside to continue the program.

The details of the C-ROB report that put AIC back in the California state budget speak to the importance of relationality. The recommendations are based on collaborative efforts between a host of named private and public entities. And behind the named collaborators is the obscured work of folks like Carlson and others who have creatively worked to keep relational channels open during the decade between AIC's official death and tentative rebirth. But of course the program could not succeed without the incarcerated writers who have been brave enough to cry in class and to have their writing published in local and national publications, the wives who have come to hear readings of their incarcerated husbands' poetry by volunteers from the Sacramento Poetry Center, and grown children who have testified at the Senate hearings about the ways AIC helped their families fight the statistical inevitability of intergenerational incarceration. And then there are the inanimate contributors: rooms with arrangeable tables and chairs; lined paper; memos authorizing the use of pencils, visiting teachers, and concerts on the yard. Whatever AIC may become, it will be because of closely tended relationships in a complex web of relations.

Carol Hinds, whom I introduced in the previous chapter, has also played a key role in the remixed reinstatement of Arts in Corrections. She is currently a member of the Inmate Family Council at California Men's Colony, where her son, Adam, was transferred in 2016. Through her advocacy work on these councils and at both state and national levels, she continues to be an important supporter of the AIC comeback.

The university where I teach has twice brought Hinds to campus as a speaker. Most recently, she was asked to speak as part of a campuswide series of events focused on Bryan Stevenson's book *Just Mercy: A Story of Justice and Redemption*. Hinds's talk was well attended, primarily by first-year and sophomore students taking prerequisite courses in the humanities. Of the seventy-four students who filled out evaluations, 90 percent were inspired to learn more about the topic and 86 percent found it helpful in their understanding of the book. Her talk was also one of the highest-rated events of the year. One first-year student from an introductory history course wrote, "This speech enriched my mind in ways I could never imagine. This is a great speech and I am grateful to you all."

Little did I know when I started working at New Folsom that I would one day have a professional relationship with a mom of someone serving a life sentence and opportunities to support her speaking from her own perspective about her and her son's experiences. I could not have imagined that I would sit in the front row of an auditorium at my university while she showed pictures of her and her son in the visiting room and talked to undergraduates about his writing process. I could not imagine these things because the lens through which I was imagining, and the rules of the system as I understood them, left no space for the pursuit of research grounded in relationship and oriented toward seeing incarcerated writers as active, sovereign members of their respective families and communities inside and outside the prison. Like many, I thought that the relational opportunities available to me as a scholar-teacher of prison writing programs fell into a binary between those sanctioned by the IRB and those likely to get me fired at the prison. My work with Hinds is helping me see that bridging can be a viable goal of prison educational justice projects and can guide what is possible at New Folsom.

Another person whose work is helping me understand the depth of the relational reality within Arts in Corrections is Peter Merts, a photographer and coauthor of *Paths of Discovery: Arts Practice and Its Impact in California Prisons* (Brewster and Merts, now in its second edition). Over the last decade, Merts has had the opportunity to photograph various AIC programs around the state. In conversation, Merts noted that the more time he spent inside with incarcerated artists, the more he wanted to find ways to make himself more personally available to the ones who were sharing their work with him. In an act of reciprocity, he began distributing the URL for his website where the families of AIC artists could find the photos he was taking. At the request of the incarcerated artists he was photographing, he also started making prints of the photos available at cost to family members through his website. As a point of reference, in 2018 families placed 50 orders for a total of 450 prints (and more than 700 total prints have been ordered since Merts created the program). Incarcerated artists have appreciated the gesture. Beautiful stories have made their way back to Merts, who has received emails from family members as far away as El Salvador thanking him for the opportunity to see their loved ones proudly displaying their work through the lens of a professional photographer. One family member emailed, "I have not been able to see my son in seven years and I cannot begin to tell you what it is like to see his laughter and all the other emotions captured, even if it is in a picture."

Of the many stories family members and AIC teachers have shared with Merts, one stands out as particularly powerful. Merts had photographed an AIC playwriting class at Donovan State Prison. The wife and son of one of the participants had viewed the class photos online, which sparked a significant conversation about race between father and son. The son was surprised to see that his dad had chosen to participate in a class that included members of different races and asked him about it. "Dad, aren't you a racist?" he asked. "Nah, son," responded the father. " I'm not racist. It's not like that in here." The son was pleased, if surprised, and told his dad about a cross-racial friendship he had been keeping secret for fear that his father would disapprove. Merts's photo, found online, allowed this incarcerated father to engage his child in an important conversation, and he was really proud that he had provided a good example for his son in this important way.

### RELATIONALITY IN THE PRESENT MOMENT: TWO CURRENT AIC PROJECTS AT NEW FOLSOM

Wilson's call for research that bridges distances has inspired the creation of two specific projects at New Folsom intended to give incarcerated students opportunities to function as literacy mentors and advocates in their own respective communities. These projects are not meant to be prescriptive. Neither are they offered as a replicable panacea for all that has been historically problematic in prison education. Rather, they add to the public record two local examples of a relational methodology in action.

### The Family Arts Program

In 2016, Carlson and I proposed the idea of a family arts (FA) program at New Folsom. The program offered three disciplinary options: iconography, classical guitar, and writing exchange.

### Iconography

The twelve-session iconography course was taught in 2017 by renowned iconographer Raymond Vincent, whose father, Robert Vincent, is a well-known guitar builder who honed his trade as an

Photo by Peter Merts.

AIC student while incarcerated (P. Brown). Students who participated in the class created their own icons using acrylic paint and
gold leaf on gesso board. Peter Merts took photos of the students'
creations that could be purchased online at cost, and artists received
permission and support from the prison to have their icons mailed
to family members.

The FA iconography class exemplifies many of the interconnected goals of the program. It was taught by an accomplished artist
whose family leveraged its connections with AIC to break the chain
of intergenerational incarceration. The work in the course supported participants as cultural assets in the communities of their choice
outside the prison and also tangibly supported the effort to make
incarcerated participants and their work more visible and accessible
to people on the outside.

Photo by Peter Merts.

*Classical Guitar*

The FA classical guitar class, taught by Gabe Becker, included weekly, ongoing instruction in classical guitar. Over the course of 2017, the FA program hosted four student recitals that included thirty-six student performances. Recitals were held in the visiting room so that family members could attend. "The families were impressed and full of smiles," wrote Becker in a year-end report on the program. "There were laughs and tears as the students each took their turn doing their solos. Afterwards, one mother expressed her delight in her son's efforts knowing how difficult it must have been for him to put in the time to practice and be able to perform for a live audience. She was happy to see this side of her son."

*Writing Exchange*

The FA writing exchange program situates participants as literacy mentors in their respective families and functionally supports participants in that role by providing them with direct instruction, curricular materials, and postage so that they can engage in a creative writing exchange with a family member of their choice on the outside (*family* being understood here in the broadest possible terms). This project does not expect incarcerated writers to be individually transformed, but rather to develop their own creative writing skills while also doing relational work that is deeply important to them. The program has been able to connect to specific political priorities within the California Governor's Office because it attends to the issue of intergenerational incarceration which has, as it should, become a serious concern for policymakers.

The FA writing exchange curriculum consists of a twenty-four-part series of nonsequential lessons that address principles of writing practice and introduce students to writers whose work reflects those principles, especially writers of color who describe and exemplify the principles of practice discussed in the curriculum series. Curricular materials come in two versions, one for adult learners (which I developed) and one for juveniles (developed by Beth Coleman, a PhD candidate at the University of North Carolina, Chapel Hill).

A nonsequential curriculum works well in prison, since the chaotic variables of the institution (lockdowns, varying levels of custody staff support, etc.) and competing obligations (work, medical appointments, etc.) makes it difficult for students to successfully commit to a tightly sequential program model. Furthermore, the lessons have been developed in such a way that participants who want to attend class but do not want to mentor anyone on the outside can still work through the curriculum. Typically, the class alternates between lessons based on writing principles from the Getting Started series and lessons based on a writer's biography from the In the Company of Writers series.

Participants take the classroom curricular materials with them to help construct their correspondence with those they are mentoring. They can either mail the materials as they are or construct their own materials using whichever pieces of the ones from the classroom they find useful. Arts in Corrections provides the envelops and postage, but participants construct their correspondence in the way that they think is best. Arts in Corrections staff do not conduct any formal screening of the material, although standard prison mailroom screening still takes place. Neither does the AIC staff require that participants share the details of any writing that they receive from their exchange partners.

Since the goal of the program is to support incarcerated people who are working to support their loved ones outside the prison— and in doing so help reduce the likelihood of intergenerational incarceration—it does not need to ask participants to construct individual narratives of personal change. Rather, participants demonstrate whether or not the program improves the rate and quality of their contact with people who they love. These quantitative and qualitative measures can be assessed without unnecessarily imposing on the privacy of the incarcerated participant. For example, one participant let me know that he shared four stories from class with his wife, who in turn found some short stories she liked and mailed them back along with a few she had written herself in response to the writing prompt. The participant reported that he and his wife were enjoying having something constructive to talk about and plan to continue participating in the program.

Because the FA writing exchange program is predicated on the idea that incarcerated participants are literacy mentors, it was important to institute a library of relevant reading material across a range of lexile levels that was culturally and linguistically diverse and that could be available both in the AIC classroom and in the visiting room at the prison. This allows participants who do not receive visitors to familiarize themselves with appropriate texts and make recommendations to their mentees through the mail or by phone. It also allows participants who do receive visitors to be familiar with relevant texts and choose appropriate material from the visiting room library when their mentees visit.

The initial library consists of fifty-five different juvenile texts across Lexile levels representing a broad range of cultural and linguistic content. There are three copies of most books available, plus ten-copy sets of nine adult texts to be used for book club–style classroom literacy projects. These additional texts represent a commitment to the literacy mentors whose mentees are adults and cover a broad range of cultural topics on issues of race, class, and gender.

In sum, the FA writing exchange currently consists of a 185-

book library that spans the three main yards at New Folsom. The library has the institutional support of both AIC program sponsors and the visiting room sergeant, who allows appropriate texts to circulate as designed. Program administrators are also considering the possibility of hosting readings in the visiting room where participants and their exchange partners can read and discuss their work.

### Collecting Relational Data on the Family Arts Program

Programs that disrupt the notion of the incarcerated student individually working toward rehabilitation or reduced recidivism can still collect quantitative data. Although the budgetary and administrative support for collecting data on this program was relatively small, a discussion about the type of data collected does offer a preliminary model for what data collected from a relational program might quantitatively measure. In 2017, both the writing exchange and iconography courses were surveyed about the type and frequency of contact they'd had with their exchange partners. Thirty-four participants completed surveys. Survey results suggest that there are both quantitative and qualitative grounds for a shift away from deficit models to justifying prison arts programs and toward models that position incarcerated people as cultural assets in their respective communities and actively support them in that role.

As indicated in Figure 1, many participants chose "Other Family Relation" when identifying their exchange partner; this category includes grandchildren, nieces, and nephews. The second highest category was "Spouse/Partner." These data indicate that projects aimed at disrupting intergenerational incarceration should consider familial relations beyond that of parent and child. Data also show that most participants communicate with their exchange partner on a monthly basis, primarily in writing (Figures 2 and 3). This rate and type of contact suggests that accelerated timelines cannot capture the literacy mentor work of participants in the program, as it will take years for incarcerated participants to establish a robust literacy mentorship with their exchange partners.[1]

The most significant data from the survey were in the form of participants' responses when asked why they had initiated the

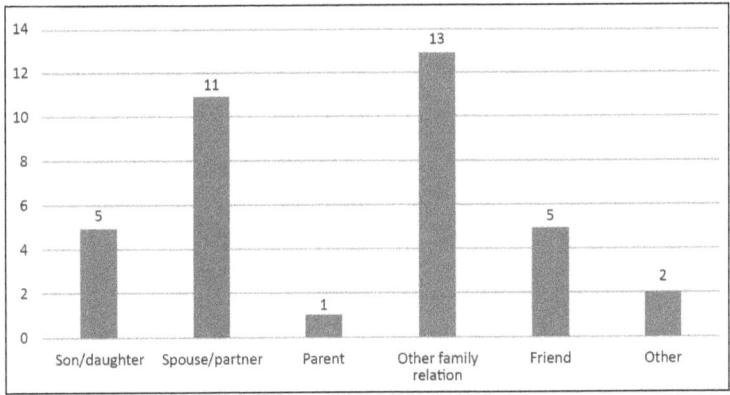

Figure 1. Types of exchange partners for inmates participating in the Family Arts program.

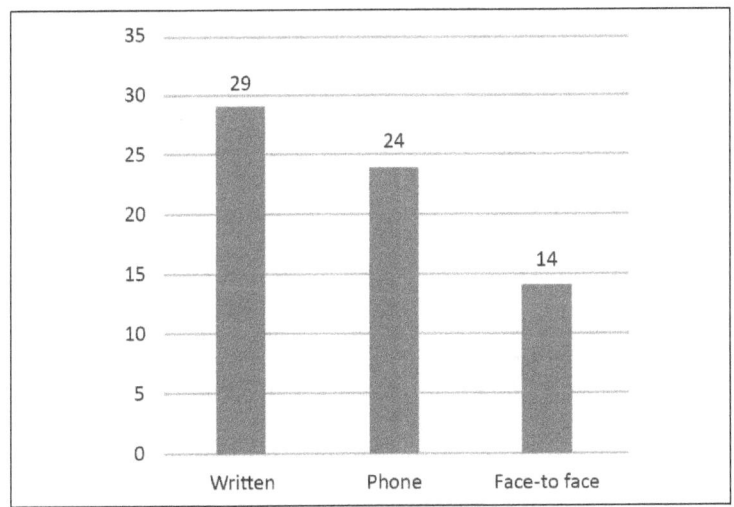

Figure 2. Types of contact between inmates and their exchange partners.

writing exchange (Figure 4). The top two responses chosen were "improved quality of contact with my exchange partner" and "to support the interpersonal (confidence, self-worth, etc.) well-being of my partner." The high number of responses in these two catego-

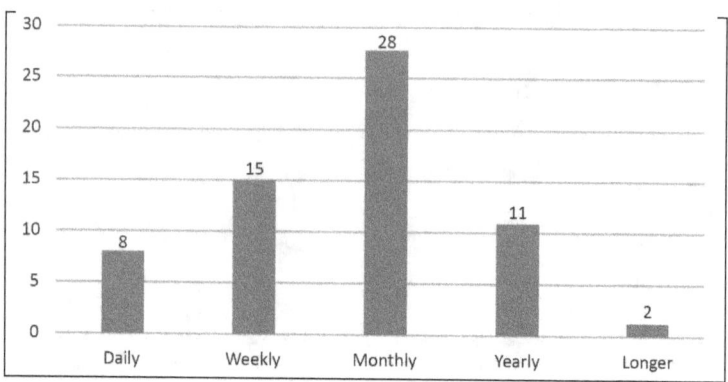

**Figure 3. Frequency of contact between participants and exchange partners.**

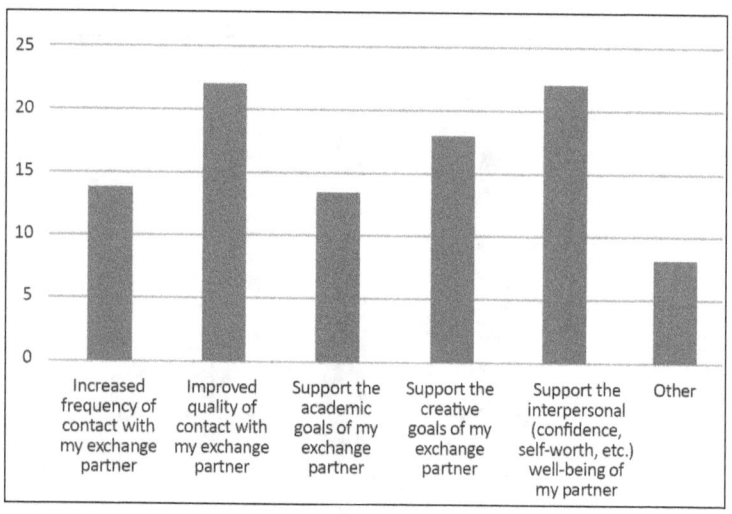

**Figure 4. Inmates' five primary goals for participating in the FA program.**

ries suggests that participants already have some relationship with their exchange partners and are looking for ways to participate with them in more meaningful ways. Similarly, in response to a question about other program goals (Figure 5), the majority of those surveyed indicated that their primary motivation for participating is to

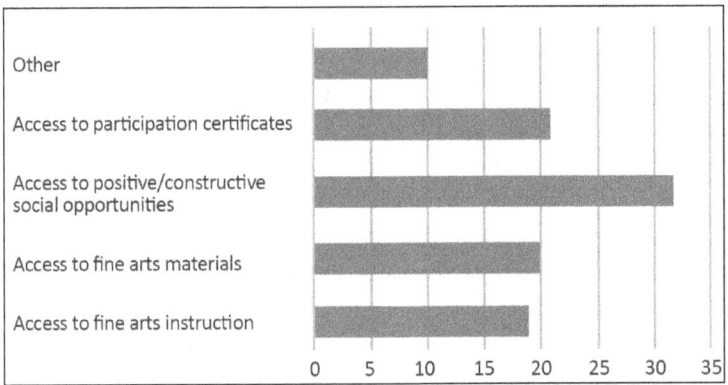

**Figure 5. Other program goals listed by incarcerated FA program participants.**

access "positive/constructive social opportunities." Taken together, these responses suggest that many incarcerated participants are already motivated to engage with their families and communities in positive ways and are looking for program opportunities that can tangibly support their intentions. This is a key shift away from a model of individual transformation.

After reviewing the survey data with participants, we noticed that the category of "Other Family Relation" (see Figure 1) masks an important pattern: namely, the choice by many participants to exchange writing with their grandchildren. The category "Grandchildren" was not included on the original survey, an oversight for which I take the responsibility, as most of the literature on intergenerational incarceration I've read addresses the parent-child relationship. Sharing the survey results with participants allowed us to discuss the reality that many of them have school-age grandchildren who might be eager to participate even if the participants' adult children are too busy with work and other obligations.

### TOGETHER WE CAN: AN INTERACTIVE DRAWING AND WRITING JOURNAL PROJECT

The Together We Can project at New Folsom came into being in 2017 when Aaché Howard-McDaniel, a student in a Principles of

Rhetoric course I was teaching at the university, proposed focusing her major project on the creation of materials to help adults talk with kids whose parents are incarcerated. Preliminary research on existing materials designed for children with incarcerated parents has revealed that some of them are primarily designed to orient children to prison. For example, *The Prison Alphabet*, written by Dr. Bahiyyah Muhammad and Muntaquim Muhammad, is a coloring book for children that uses the alphabet as a framework to build a vocabulary about incarceration presumably to help children understand and communicate with and about their incarcerated loved ones. The coloring book begins with "A is for Arrest" and ends with "Z is for Zoo."

Howard-McDaniel and many incarcerated artists at New Folsom feel that such a focus might have the unintended consequence of normalizing prison and perpetuating stereotypes about both the place and the people who live inside. When presented with *The Prison Alphabet*, AIC participants noticed that the book recirculated racist notions of incarceration and policing. They also noted that many of the illustrations infantilized and even dehumanized incarcerated people. For example, the drawing of the officer on the "A is for Arrest" page has typically Caucasian features while most of the drawing of incarcerated people have features more closely associated with people of color. The "Q is for Quiet Time" page shows an incarcerated person on their bunk with a correctional officer holding his pointer finger to his mouth to suggest that no talking is allowed. Similarly, "S is for Schedule" has a drawing and caption showing that incarcerated people "Play outside in the yard" at 4 o'clock. And the "Z is for Zoo" page makes a direct connection between incarcerated people and caged animals.

In October 2017, I met with three existing AIC classes to brainstorm possible alternatives to the existing materials available to children. Together we decided that AIC's creative writing and visual arts classes at New Folsom would work alongside Howard-McDaniel to create a children's drawing and writing journal primarily designed to foster relationship-building between incarcerated people and their children through the arts. The group decided that individual questions about incarceration are best answered directly by people who have a relationship with their child rather than through mass-produced materials that risk overgeneralizing about or demeaning incarcerated people. We delivered first drafts to Howard-McDaniel, who used them to design questions for a focus group of young adults who had grown up with at least one incarcerated parent.

Howard-McDaniel then came with me to New Folsom to discuss the results of her focus group with the incarcerated artists working on the journal. She had collected some heart-wrenching perspectives about what it was like to grow up with an incarcerated parent. The in-class conversations surrounding her findings were intense and often raw, as incarcerated parents countered the narratives Howard-McDaniel had collected with their own stories, mostly about frustration and loss. Those conversations deeply informed the in-class conversation during which thematic and design decisions about the project were made.

The AIC classes chose the name Together We Can for the project and determined that the journal could accommodate secondary goals of increasing a child's confidence, academic vocabulary, and self-reflection and persistence toward personal goals. Those secondary goals are reflected in the ten drawing and writing topics that the group settled on: teach each other, build, aspire, figure it out, overcome, play and have fun, dream, fly, cry when we're sad, talk, and listen. The topic list is a curious mix of relational and aspirational themes that reflect the complexity of what the AIC class members want to communicate to the children in their lives.

Twenty-six AIC participants provided design and editorial support for the project through multiple drafts. Three participants took the extra step of responding to a second draft of the journal and were named as contributing authors. In particular, Saahdi Coleman contributed both a preface and a poem addressed directly to children. Coleman wrote:

> We made this book to remind you that you are strong, smart, and special; that you can do anything you want as long as you keep trying. We made this book to remind you that it's okay to be a kid—to play and have fun, to cry when you are sad, and to dream big.

We made this book so you know that we are thinking about you as much as you are thinking about us. We made this book to encourage you to do your best in school because grown-ups can learn from kids too. We made this book so that we can stay connected and so we can build a relationship that makes us both happy. We made this book for you.

Howard-McDaniel also included a preface from her perspective addressing her young audience directly:

I was once that little girl wondering why my father was not around, not feeling good enough to keep him around when I did see him. I always wondered, if I was a "good kid," would he still leave? I constantly asked myself if he really loved me, although my mother always tried to convince me that he did. It was a constant battle between hate and self-doubt. Not even knowing what either was, all I knew was that I felt those things. If I could go back in time and speak to my younger self, I would have a lot to say.

I would tell myself, "You are loved" and that it takes a lot of love to love someone from so far away. That's unconditional love. I would tell myself, "You are special and you are enough." I would tell myself not to grow up too fast, enjoy being a kid, let the adults worry about the adult things. I would tell myself, "You are not an outsider. Don't feel alone when you see the other kids with their fathers, you are just as important as those kids." I would tell myself that I was not the problem.

I would tell myself, your future is bright, to keep your head up and continue to work towards what you want in life. I would tell myself that you are not defined by the environment you're growing up in, you are not confined, you are a leader. You will choose one day to be different and not follow behind the footsteps of those you grew up around.

You are not a square, you are not soft, you are not a statistic. You are destined for greatness. You are smart, kind, loved, wanted, and highly capable. Dream big, and never give up on what you want it life. Stay strong, you got this!

Using grant funds, we printed 1,500 copies of the journal. In February 2018, copies of the journals were distributed to AIC participants and we began working with the visiting room sergeant on an appropriate protocol for making the journals widely available for free in the room. A few months later, Howard-McDaniel returned to New Folsom to talk with participants about how the journals were being received and to initiate a follow-up project focused on using digital spaces and tools to facilitate deeper connections between incarcerated people and their families. During that class meeting, one participant shared that his eight-year-old daughter loved the journal and that they had spent two hours writing and coloring together during her last visit. Then he turned directly to Howard-McDaniel and thanked her for including her own narrative in the journal. He recalled that as he was reading Howard-McDaniel's words to his daughter she kept interrupting to say, "That is how I feel." He said that his daughter had never talked about her feelings about incarceration because she did not have the words to do so. He credited Howard-McDaniel with opening up a conversation between him and his daughter that allowed her to voice her feelings and, in the process, allowed him to provide comfort and support to her. Another participant shared photos of his grandson coloring in the journal. He was smiling widely as he recalled that his grandson thought the journal "was cool" and was proud of his grandpa for making it.

In the year-end grant report submitted to the William James Association, Howard-McDaniel had this to say about her experience collaborating on the project:

> While thinking of ways I could help children of the incarcerated, I went in knowing I wanted to make a difference. Once upon a time I was that child and, in a sense, I still am. In response, I felt like I wanted to help with that process of figuring it out. I wanted to give back. It turned into something I became very passionate about. I thought the "why" would've helped me understand why my father was in and out of prison, but after talking to the men inside I learned that I just want and needed a connection, a relationship. The coloring

book idea changed from educating the child on prison and how it works to helping the child feel connected to their parent, loved, and cared about even if they don't see them every day.

Surprisingly, visiting Folsom was my first prison experience. It made all of this very real for me, which is why I think I never visited my own father. I didn't want it to be a reality, so I never was eager to visit him. After listening to some of the stories these men shared with me, I started to wonder if I could have done more and if I put too much of the blame on my father since I am on the outside and I have more resources.

Overall, this project has given me a different view of the situation. It allowed me to see that even though I understand the US prison system now, I am still that little girl missing the presence of a father figure. This project has motivated me to start a relationship with my father, which I am beyond grateful for. I actually went in with this idea that I would be helping some child get through this, but in return, I came out helping and learning more about myself and my experience with this issue.

We expect to be able to gather quantitative and qualitative information about the project without expecting participants to generate transformational narratives or share private or sacred knowledge. Whereas the Family Arts program expanded the relational circle at New Folsom by situating incarcerated students as literacy mentors in their own spheres of influence, the Together We Can project broadens the circle even more by including people with incarcerated family members as both project initiators and coauthors (Howard-McDaniel) and as co-creators of meaning (the children who use the journal). In one last addition to the circle, Howard-McDaniel and I put together a panel for the 2018 National Race and Pedagogy Conference at the University of Puget Sound that included her mother, who spoke to the issues the project raised from the perspective of the parent on the outside.

## ANALYZING AIC PROJECTS USING THE RELATIONAL INTERPRETIVE FRAMEWORK

Both the FA writing exchange program and the Together We Can project were designed according to the framework I adapted from the work of Margaret Kovach, discussed in detail in Chapter 3. Here, I apply each of the framework's five main elements to analyzing both projects.

**Decolonial Intention and Ethics.** *This element asks the researcher to examine how both individuals and groups have been affected by and complicit in colonial legacies and to ask questions that challenge Western knowledge systems.*

In the case of both projects, one driving question was whether a sponsor-scholar might challenge individuated, primarily economic measures for evaluating program value. When the autonomous individual no longer has primacy in a research methodology, researchers can pay closer attention to and account for the complicated and interrelated elements that were already part of any individual's story. Furthermore, freed of the operational assumption that human subjects exist on a linear plane, researchers can focus on incarcerated participants as members of existing relational communities and study and/or support participants' movements deeper into those communities. For scholars interested in employing decolonial methodologies, being mindful and strategic about what a research project sets out to measure is crucial. As Shawn Wilson notes, "research is about unanswered questions, but it also reveals our unquestioned answers" (6).

**Researcher Preparation.** *This aspect of the framework asks researchers to explore their own relationship to the research or project, finding and making sense of the memories and stories that inform their motivation for the work (Hampton).*

When I first began working at New Folsom, Marty Williams made a comment about incarcerated people not needing to be fixed or saved. This idea became a north star to me, guiding my work on all future AIC projects. Nevertheless, it took me years to reconcile

Williams's wise words with project ideas that actually embodied them, as the story of my failed study makes painfully clear. Between Williams's comment and these two recent projects were years of teaching and studying during which my teacherly intention and practice only gradually became aligned. And of course, this is still an unfinished (and unfinishable) business. Furthermore, the secondhand memory of the juggling student who said teaching his kid to juggle made him feel like a dad for the first time (see p. 39) reminds me that incarcerated people are often denied the tools and opportunities to do what they already want to do: participate positively in their communities.

Before and during both of the AIC projects discussed in this chapter, I have had to be mindful of my familial relationship to this work. As I've made clear, I was first invited to the prison by my father at a time of crisis in his life and the life of Arts in Corrections. He continues to be an integral part of any work I do at the prison, and his ethos has opened administrative doors at New Folsom that I know would have otherwise been tightly closed to me. Beyond the access that I have been afforded as his daughter, I am also mindful of the way whiteness often further increases my access and mobility in the system. I know that in my case I have not had to wonder, as my colleague Henry Robinette has, whether the actions of unhelpful correctional officers are motivated by racism or resentment (Carnes).

**Community Accountability.** *This aspect of the framework asks researchers to demonstrate how the project responds to the articulated needs and/or desires of the community, evolves in response to community feedback, and is terminated when or if the community decides that the project is at odds with its health and sovereignty.*

Both projects respond directly to the stories AIC participants have shared over the years about why they participate in AIC and how their participation effects their relationships with their families and/or other people outside the prison. One story, usually told by Carol Hinds, stands out as an unexpected outcome of connecting the AIC classroom with visitors to the prison. In Hinds's telling, a man named Jacob saw the inside of the visiting room for the first time when he went there to perform as part of a classical guitar recital. In his seventeen years of incarceration, nobody had ever come to visit him. Being in the room for the first time was emotionally overwhelming, but Jacob managed to finish the recital. The experience of seeing families interacting in that space inspired Jacob to begin the process of locating his mother with whom he had not had any contact in more than twenty years. Jacob now communicates regularly with his mother and sisters. Beyond reconnecting with his family on the outside, Jacob has also moved into the role of guitar teacher with AIC and has either participated in or overseen ten recitals in the same visiting room where he first played his guitar. The visiting room was also the site for Jacob's solo recital, which was attended by incarcerated people, prison administrators, and visitors from the community. Jacob's story is a strong example of how AIC at New Folsom works to be accountable to the articulated desires of incarcerated artists. It also exemplifies the reciprocal quality of that accountability in the way that Jacob leveraged the opportunities provided by the program to broaden and strengthen his own web or relations inside and outside the prison.

Besides responding directly to the articulated desires of AIC participants, both of these projects are constructed in such a way that participants have sovereignty over how they employ and or adapt them. In the case of the Family Arts program, curricular materials are provided directly to incarcerated participants so that they can amend and/or adapt those materials in their respective mentoring processes. Furthermore, participants can determine their own level of participation. They can also decide when to stop participating and are allowed to retain any of the materials they have acquired up until the point that they voluntarily terminate their participation.

In the case of the Together We Can project, incarcerated participants have full control over the distribution and use of the materials that were created. They are responsible for helping interested family members acquire the journal (either directly from them or through the visiting room program). Furthermore, if a time came when participants found that the journals were causing more harm than good, we would, as a group, determine whether to terminate the program. A respect for sovereignty has precedent within AIC at New Folsom. Over the years, classes have been added and/or teacher contracts have been allowed to run out based on feedback from participants.

**Reciprocity/Community Benefit.** *The fourth aspect of the framework asks the researcher to design a project in such a way that it respects participants as already valuable members of their respective communities and directly works to support community members in those existing roles. Benefits to the community, made primarily by the community members themselves, are part of the clearly articulated outcomes of the research project.*

Whereas the accountability element focuses on the structures that govern how a project begins, evolves, and ends, the primary focus of this aspect of the framework is an attention to the types of outcomes the project generates. The FA program works to support participants as literacy mentors and does not overly determine how they "recruit" their mentees or micromanage how that mentor-mentee relationship progresses. The program's administrative structures are invisible to the mentee. Incarcerated mentors are the agents of action in the program; the onus is on them to make a contribution to their community. Similarly, the Together We Can project positions incarcerated participants as the locus of potential community benefit. As was evident in the stories of fathers and grandfathers sharing the journals with their families, the appreciation for the journals and the quality of contact are centered around the contributions of the incarcerated community members.

**Knowledge Gathering/Meaning-Making.** *The final aspect of the framework asks that the types of knowledge gathered though the project and the meanings that are constructed about that knowledge privilege the community rather than the individual as the unit of analysis, balance a need for data with a respect for participants' desire to protect sacred and/or private knowledge, and directly include the communi-*

*ty in the process of meaning-making and subsequent distribution of knowledge.*

The FA program does not require participants to write about their participation or submit examples of the work they either send or receive from their writing partners (although all participants may have the opportunity to submit work for a future anthology). By focusing on the rate and quality of contact, the program demonstrates its value without requiring the participants to divulge private or sacred knowledge. Together We Can, too, works to respect private or sacred knowledge: the writings and drawings in the journals are not shared with program administrators. Of course, writing and drawing that happens in the visiting room is subject to the oversight of relevant custody staff to the same degree as everything else that happens there; although we cannot predict or control for those potential encounters, we do work directly with the visiting sergeant to ensure that the project has administrative support. At the present time, children are allowed to bring their journals in and out of the visiting room, and these journals will be processed with the same level of scrutiny as other materials (such as homework) that children are encouraged to bring and work on with incarcerated family members.

### CONCLUSION: AN INVITATION TO JOIN THE WORK ALREADY UNDER WAY

Framing prison literacy work with the essential self-reflective questions of *what* and *with/for whom* has already begun to open up space in the scholarship for a more critical attention to our own complicity in the communities with or on whose behalf we have attempted to work. To expand on these essential questions, I have attempted to add my own story of confusing good intention with ethical, relational work and pointed out the ways that the colonial logics underwriting Western research methodologies still make it difficult for committed scholars to enact truly decolonial projects. I have tried to show how relationality functions within the AIC program at New Folsom for the purpose of adding my voice to the conversation about what is real and how we know it to be such.

And I have worked to demonstrate how a few current AIC projects have been born using an interpretive framework based on the work of Margaret Kovach.

In all of this, I am reminded of the words of Malea Powell: "Though I have questioned my own implicatedness at every stage of this project, I suspect that, in the end, I have not been suspicious enough" ("Blood" 3). The work currently happening at New Folsom gives me hope that scholar-teachers working in the prison can, through a careful attention to methodology, better align intention and practice. But this small hope is couched in a grand despair regarding the ways race and class (in particular) continue to be criminalized. A sharp critique of the broader system does, in very real ways, diminish any gains that seem to be made in programs like Arts in Corrections. And the critique of prison educators as torchbearers of dehumanizing neoliberal policy makes the complicity of scholar-teachers like me painfully clear. I believe, though that, on balance, to walk away from the incarcerated students at New Folsom under the auspice of an unresolvable complicity with the system would be an ironic and egregious show of privilege. Many of the incarcerated writers and artists I know at New Folsom will not walk out. I think about that every time I do, and that reality keeps me coming back, listening for ways that I can support their desire to be recognized as assets and contributors to communities inside and outside the prison.

Because Arts in Corrections, particularly at New Folsom, has been the site of amazing, albeit small and local, ruptures in the status quo of life inside, it has provided a fruitful context for the arguments made in this book. And, as has been demonstrated, what made AIC such a successful program during its thirty-year tenure was its foundational understanding that "rather than introducing a cultural community in prison, [Artist Facilitators] were joining one" (Cleveland, *Art* 59). Making opportunities the primary goal of the program permitted AIC to act with some level of sovereignty and flexible invention at each institution—some institutions built up programs that privileged writing, others focused on visual or performing arts, and still others, like New Folsom over the last twenty years, followed the interest of both incarcerated participants and outside community members in building a strong music program. In each case, AIC programs organically followed the strongest relational threads to build contingent programs that met a host of articulated needs and desires.

What I do not suggest in this book are specific ways for scholar-teachers to meet the demands of their individual institutions and their corresponding structures of professional advancement. This is not an oversight. Of course, scholar-teachers employed by academic institutions have quotas and pressures to publish. Nonetheless, these unavoidable structural demands to which we consent cannot be drivers in the creation or sustaining of community projects because, as Blackburn and Cushman point out, in such instances the end of the project signals the end of the relationship between the university and the community. And, I would add, situations where project termination is concomitant with a severing of relational ties carry a distinct and dangerous colonial possibility.

In the context of my work at New Folsom, it has been important to recognize and respect the web of relations that are always present in and around the prison classroom. It has also been important to remember that my relationship with the prison in general and AIC more specifically is contingent. Funding comes and goes. There are lockdowns and yard recalls. A change in the protocol to midday count cuts the time available for class in half.

And then there is the truth that when I am at New Folsom I am only ever a visitor. At the end of the day, I submit my manila-colored card to the officer at the main gate, sign out, put my driver's license back in my wallet and dig in my purse for my car keys as I wait for a break in the stream of vehicles carrying second-watch custody staff away from the prison to wherever they go. Sometimes I cry when I am driving away. Other times I turn up the music and roll the windows down. But however I go, I always leave. And that inevitable leaving must fundamentally inform what I do when I am inside. To the extent that prison scholar-teachers orient their work around an individuated, economic value of writing, we do colonial work that does not respect or serve communities of incarcerated students. And, as Williams reminds me often, incarcerated communities do not need serving in the ways that outsiders often imagine it anyway. But they might just welcome relational methodologies that can describe and sustain the work already under way.

# WRITERS AND TEACHERS, PART 5

**Family**

I was born into a tug of war of cultures.
I am a full blood Native American, of the Mescalero Apache
    Nation.
I was born from a clan and to a clan.
I was born with and for the traditions and ceremonies of my
    people.
These ways are in my blood and part of my heart, mind, and
    spirit.
This is what I was born from.
But unfortunately what I was raised with was contrary
to what I was born for.

My dad was former Marine turned trucker/biker.
On the road most of the time, whether it was on
eighteen wheels or two, it didn't really matter.
A damn good provider, a half-way decent father,
and horrible husband.
At home I was surrounded by sex, drugs, violence,
and random fits of paranoia.
At school I took everything I learned at home and
applied it to my peers and teachers,
disrespecting the women who were trying to teach me
and using violence to satisfy my lust for power over my peers.

Mom pretended to be oblivious to what was going on,
but at night prayed for her sons.

As I got older I promised myself that I'd play
the game harder and better than Pops.

My elders always told me that if I kept playing,
this game would end in prison or death.
It appears that I've won since I hold my 5-digit prize.

So why does it feel like I've lost?

—Andrew Molino

**Sing Me a Song**

vs. 1

> SING ME A SONG ABOUT MORNINGS
> 'BOUT BIRDS SINGING SWEET AS THEY WAKE
> SING ME A SONG OF BEGINNINGS
> SING A JOURNEY MY HEART CAN TAKE

vs. 2

> SING ME A SONG ABOUT NOONTIMES
> 'BOUT THE SUN SHINING HIGH IN THE SKY
> SING ME A SONG OF THE MIDDLE OF THINGS
> SING WINGS SO MY HEART CAN FLY

vs. 3

> SING ME A SONG ABOUT SUNSETS
> 'BOUT THE SUN SINKING LOW IN THE WEST
> SING ME A SONG ABOUT ENDINGS
> SING MY HEART HOME TO ITS REST

BRIDGE

> SING OF SPRINGTIME AND SUMMER, TELL ME OF
>     FALL
> SING OF THE SEASONS, SING OF THEM ALL
> SING OF THE WEATHER, RAIN FOG AND MIST
> DON'T FORGET WINTER, THE LAST ON THE LIST

vs. 4

> SING ME A SONG ABOUT NIGHT TIMES
> WHEN THE MOON AND THE STARS DANCE AND
>     PLAY
> SING ME A SONG ABOUT DARKNESS
> SING THE DARKNESS THAT BRINGS A NEW DAY

—Ken Blackburn

## The Tier Tender

*Part One*

The writing group meets in the windowless prison library. Behind the swinging counter door, twice labeled "Out of Bounds," stand two walls lined with thick, gold-foiled law books. To the left, bulky computer stations—dead-eyed sentinels—guard the stacks full of the books that require less permission. Someone comes in quietly, turns his body to thread the space between the antiquated machines, disappears between the shelves, pulls a book out as careful as if it were a redwood sliver in his palm, and leaves without a sound.

Between the "Out of Bounds" law books and the sleepy computers we push together four heavy tables that shudder and squeal in protest. I kick a rusted, buckled table leg back into position and run my hand over the Formica wood grain. This is the second meeting of the newly formed writer's group in A Facility, the second time we have come intending to raise our voices in the library.

The library clerk hands off the ducat with each man's California Department of Corrections number and housing assignment to someone who is allowed to use the phone. Ten minutes after the call to the Blocks, men swagger in, slow and purposeful, from work or from their Houses. The room begins to buzz with Muses recently welcomed.

To my left, Red Beard—Portland glasses, creaseless grey baseball cap—taps his Composition book. I saw him earlier so I already know that four hours of last night were given to the task and he likes the words that rolled from his pen. Across from him will sit the tall man—light skinned, two-inch grey beard in proportion to the afro that will be his crown when he later reads for the group through smoky melamine glasses that now hang around his neck taped on one side to their shoestring cord. The glasses swing away from his body in rhythm with his right foot as he pushes his walker to the table and arranges his things.

The air smells of promise, connection, things that are alive. But death works the corners, peeks from behind the bookshelves, loops around our ankles, eventually enters the conversation. On the far wall, behind the well-spoken man with a close fade who will be the group's leader, are photocopies of the 8x10 poster an administrator has taped up in the hallways of all three facilities. The posters are side-by-side, in English and Spanish, with this helpful advice for those considering suicide:

"Are you or someone you know . . .
THINKING ABOUT
SUICIDE?
*With help comes hope!*
HONOR YOUR LIFE
*Talk to any staff member now!"*

In the original colored version, suspended, armless peachy hands without crease or wrinkle reach towards each other in the middle of the page. Since these are photocopies the hands are grey, morgue-ish. Suicide in prison is a liability to be avoided. Homicide is not exactly welcomed either but is much easier to document. Either way, the law requires that every body that leaves New Folsom goes to the Coroner for one last carve up, one last thorough violence to determine what exactly happened. And the rules also require that all dead men leave in handcuffs.

Somehow we come around to Compassionate Release. "They do that?" I ask. There are mixed responses—head shake YES and NO, there is talk of rules, technicalities. A white guy about my age with tattoo sleeves down to the cuffs, holds up a single finger. "I've seen it *one* time. And the guy had lots of money." He speaks with authority on the matter, considers my question an invitation to talk about other things he has seen. "We have a guy right now, been battling Cancer for seven years all by himself. And there was another guy who they gave six months, but he made it three years." He looks around for someone to validate the remembrance; I think about the cruel and arbitrary relationship between life and numbers here. He tells me how he has become so familiar with Cancer sentences.

"I'm a tier tender over in the Correctional Treatment Center [CTC]."

I haven't been so he explains that the Treatment Center is a cell-block reserved for the terminally ill. Cellblocks at New Folsom are shaped like a slice of pie with the guard tower looking out from the Panoptic center over the arc of the two-story tier. The concrete tiers in the mainline blocks are always kept clear; the tiers at the CTC are crowded with IV polls, blood pressure cuffs, sterilized medical paraphernalia—trappings of a supervised first-world death. The common area between the guard tower and tier has been converted, steel picnic tables making way for cramped clusters of desks and workstations brought in for the doctors and nurses. The CTC smells—Medicine, latex, sweat, bodies that can't or won't shower, pine forest disinfectant that never really lifts the stains from where the incarcerated dying leave notes written in excrement.

"What does a tier tender do?" I ask.

"I clean up vomit and well . . ." He unclasps his hands to hold up the remaining invisible words. The respect with which he speaks, suggests he is more gentle escort and witness than janitor.

"What is that like?" I ask, the second half of my sentence falling into a whisper.

He looks down, through the table, into the deep hole opened up by the moment. "It can be real hard. And I don't mean the vomit."

Everyone has arrived now, we start class, read aloud, and comment on each other's work.

*Part Two*

The Tier Tender is taking Gabe's classical guitar class. On the first day Gabe spent the allotted time talking about how to stand with a guitar, how to sit with a guitar, and how to make the transition between standing and sitting. The class has been meeting for six months, two hour stretches on Monday afternoons. Eight guys come regularly, bring their own guitars.

The week before Christmas the Tier Tender lost someone. His family came to Visiting so they could mourn together. In an act without precedent, everyone who needed to signed the form that allowed him to bring his guitar. He played it in his grief, in the circle of his family. He knew how to move from standing to sitting.

—Anna Plemons

# Afterword: Ethics and Implications: A Discussion with an Author, an Editor, and an Indigenous Scholar

Anna Plemons, Steve Parks, and Kristin L. Arola

THIS IS STEVE SPEAKING, CURRENT editor of the Studies in Writing and Rhetoric series. One of the visions for the SWR series was to publish work that engaged with the ethics of scholarship and disciplinary practice. Among the elements of this project that fascinated me as an editor was the drawing together of Indigenous and decolonial theories as a way to reframe the work of prison literacy programs, specifically with individuals of diverse background. My sense was that the project posed the ethical question of what it means to invoke such theories to study programs and populations that emerged from different historical trajectories (though this book does show a continuity between mass incarceration and colonialism). The situation grows even more complex when the author is a white middle-class woman. Issues of appropriation, for instance, begin to emerge. The act of navigating such terrain in the hopes of articulating a more just version of prison literacy was a fraught enterprise.

Beyond the specifics of the project, the field as a whole is navigating these issues—listening to what Indigenous scholars have to say about how to learn (and not appropriate) such methodologies; how to enact (and not make just a metaphor) the goals of decoloniality. This book provides a case study of that complexity and an attempt to navigate a pathway forward. With that in mind, I asked the author, Anna Plemons, and Indigenous scholar Kristin Arola (who wrote the book's foreword) to have a conversation about these issues.

**STEVE PARKS:** I want to begin by thanking each of you for taking part in this conversation. Particularly you, Anna. It is so in the collaborative spirit of scholarship to share the backstory to the writing of this book.

I'm not sure there is an ideal place to begin, so maybe just getting some key terms out might be useful. Throughout the book, the reader will see terms like *Indigenous, postcolonial,* and *decolonial.* How did you understand and approach those terms in your work?

**ANNA PLEMONS:** I think it's important to articulate the idea that Indigenous theory is distinct from coloniality, even as Indigenous theory can be used to critique coloniality. It is not postcolonial because Indigenous theory was before, and it was during, and it is after the various colonial projects that have marred global history. For me, there is a relationship there. Maybe it is "post" in my thinking, because I came through traditional Western schooling and to Indigenous theory fairly recently, but the relationship between Indigenous theory and postcoloniality isn't teleological. The former does not follow or remedy the latter. Indigenous theory articulates ways of knowing that are wholly independent from coloniality.

**STEVE:** I'm just wondering, Kristin, as someone who's done work across those terms, how do you think about the way in which the field can bring in Indigenous methodologies? What are some of the ethical concerns that authors would need to take into account? Here I'm thinking of conversations with Anna on this very topic during the writing of this book.

**KRISTIN AROLA:** I struggle with that all the time. I present on it a lot because I don't know the answer. I'm always trying to work it out. But from where I sit right now, which may not be the answer, if an Indigenous scholar has published something, they most likely know, and maybe even hope, that others will take it up and use it. Cite it and do work with it. That's not to say that that work is necessarily going to be ethical. But if it's out there, and I've heard Malea Powell say this before, then use it, cite it. We wouldn't write and we wouldn't publish, if we didn't want to share our ideas. That being said, I see a few challenges here.

First, and this is a big one, when cultural rhetoric as a subdiscipline starts to enact story as theory in scholarship, there are some things that I don't feel comfortable with other people using. So, for example, I told a story about the connection between thunderbirds and eagles in Ojibwa culture. I did this for a particular reason in a particular presentation. But I don't feel great about someone not connected to the culture citing that knowledge. I told that story for a reason in that moment because it was my way of seeing through something, and while I hope it helps you see something too (or I wouldn't have shared it), you probably have your own stories, your own traditions, your own ways of coming to knowing and coming to make sense of things. I used mine, you use yours. I see that this flies in the face of my comment "if it's published, use it" (as this discussion itself will be published). So, second, we all need to question the ethics in citation practices. Is everything ours to cite? What is and what isn't? Where/when does that line get crossed? In watching Anna draft this book, I saw her grapple with this a lot, specifically around the question of, "Is it okay for a white person to use Indigenous theory? To what ends? And is it okay to use it if they're using the theory to talk about non-Indigenous people?"

STEVE: The use of Indigenous theory to study diverse populations was actually touched upon by a reviewer. The reviewer had real concerns about exactly what you, Kristin, brought up just now. So, Anna, how did you sort through those questions around your identity? How did you come to understand the ethics of using Indigenous methodologies in this project?

ANNA: Slowly. And, to be honest, with some trepidation because I really respect each of those questions and understand why they're important questions that should be asked every time white scholars attempt to use Indigenous theory. These questions were asked of me, and if I was reviewing the manuscript, I would have asked them too. So I want to respond, but not in a defensive way. I think what I came to, in part, like Kristin was saying—and here I am thinking of Zoe Todd's work, too—is that if somebody has taken the time to add their voice to the public record, and it's good scholarship, and it can shape our understanding and engagement with the world, then it should be taken seriously. If it seems like the right frame for a situation, then it's worth asking the next question, which is always, "Can I use this in a way that is ethical?"

And I think, for me, the context of prison complicates the question of ethical use in important ways. I wonder if it makes any sense to use deeply Western methodologies to discuss a problem that very much belongs to the West. The American prison is a crisis that came to be in a very Western space. And, so, in trying to engage it in a critical way, I just think of Audre Lorde's question: Are the tools needed to think about this issue in a productive way already in the toolbox? The frame through which we look at things absolutely matters and, in many ways, determines what we see. Here I am thinking of the V. F. Cordova quote about the snowball: The present shape affects the future shape. So, it absolutely matters what methodology we use now because they will shape the conversation we are able to have ten years from now.

STEVE: To build on that point, I think both of you sort of mentioned the importance of how the author positions themselves to the work. I'm just wondering if there were moments as a writer (Anna) or reader (Kristin) where this issue stood out. A moment where the complications seemed overwhelming. A moment where you discovered, through revising, a stance that seemed a productive path forward.

KRISTIN: One of the things I noticed as a reviewer was that Anna's first draft started by being overly apologetic. The story was driven explicitly by the question "I am a white woman and I'm doing this, is this okay? Is this okay? Is this okay? Is this okay?" This repetition really took over. I was grateful she was coming from that place in the process, and I think it's important for people to know she was coming from that place in the process. But at a certain point, when you spend that much energy apologizing for your embodiment, you kind of take away from illustrating what these methodologies can do and what these methodologies are good for doing. I liked that she pivoted from sheer apology to a stance that is more like "Hey, I'm a white lady, I'm using this theory for a reason, I come to it with a good heart, but I am also open to listening and being told that this isn't OK." That stance was important to me.

STEVE: My sense is there are a lot of apologies out there that once made, don't actually change any practices. I don't think that is true of your book. Still, I am wondering, why was your initial response to apologize for use? How did you think through that different position of recognizing embodiment but not shutting down using the theory for hopefully positive structural change?

ANNA: I appreciate what you're saying. I also find it distasteful when apology is the prelude to more of the same. I appreciate the way you've articulated that. And you are right. That's not what I want to do. I want to create space for a conversation about prison education and educational justice and that objective is going to require some disruption of ideological business as usual. The way I have been thinking about it lately is this: If mass incarceration is a social justice issue, then it flat-out requires an intervention that is itself socially just. Full stop.

I do feel like I did a lot of apologizing and I still don't really know how to do it differently, if I am being honest. I am happy that some of those apologetic contortions got edited out, so that the text could stay focused on the methodology and not the angst of the writer. But I don't know how I would've done it differently because I don't think it's appropriate just to come marching in and be like, "I read two books and now I've got something to say." I think it's appropriate to work through those things with some respect. Here I am thinking of Kristin's work on slow composition. I think it is important to move slowly and mindfully and be honest about one's positioning. It doesn't seem appropriate to just go barging in. But it's probably also not cool to expect reviewers and editors to absolve white scholars of their totally appropriate apprehensions. So, I don't know where that leaves us.

STEVE: Kristin, you were shaking your head a lot during that answer. What were you thinking?

KRISTIN: Her words really resonated with me, in part as I'm seeing this move in the field lately—at least in rhetorical studies where folks who do (or trend towards) object-oriented rhetoric, posthumanism, new materialism, and affect studies are starting to look to Indigenous theory and thinking like, "Okay, maybe we did colonize that a little bit. So how do we do this work better?" So, I'm grateful that is happening, but at the same time I'm nervous. I'm nervous that it's going to do exactly what Anna just said, that move of, "Okay, I read the three books Kristin kept yelling at me to read and now I'm going to drop some Indigenous knowledge." No, please, don't do that. I want someone to engage but I want them to do it authentically and ethically, from a place of being unsure: "I'm not sure, here's what I've read. Here's what I'm thinking. I'm thinking this might help us in these ways."

STEVE: In some ways the argument of "you should do your research first" should be true of anybody who enters any new methodology. So I sometimes hear the fear . . . that there's an assumption that we can just jump in and grab Indigenous scholarship and use it without that care and respect. That we can do that without consequence. And I'm wondering if that is part of your fear. That this easy running over and grabbing the theory to fit into the moment, the latest trend, is going to reduce its intended impact. And what would the bad version of this book be in your mind, Kristin? I'm not going to ask Anna to answer, since that seems oddly cruel somehow, but what would be the worst-case scenario?

KRISTIN: That's a good question. The worst case for me would have been for her to use the theory she's using, but in a way that was solely for the good of making a name for herself. If it didn't have any ends that were relational in nature, communal in nature, had any social justice, decolonial implications at the end of it. If her engagement with relationality was just a "Hey, here's some slick progressive theory. I used it! look at me, look at me, look at me!" Worst case is using it to one's own ends because, then, what was the point in the first place?

**STEVE:** My example of this is that no matter what the theory is invoked, it seems to me we still ended up grading papers for standard English. [*Ed.:* See Asao Inoue's recent talk or the work of Vershawn Young for powerful countermodels.] I think what you're saying is the best version of a book like this one might be where it uses the theory to argue for a much different paradigm, something that doesn't reinforce what is already there.

**KRISTIN:** Yeah, absolutely.

**STEVE:** Of course, such a perfect book probably doesn't exist. So the question becomes how an author navigates such goals in the materiality of their practice, their own embodiment. With the book done, are there areas, Anna, that you think "I did my best, but I'm still trying to navigate this particular issue, positionality?"

**ANNA:** Absolutely. When I think about it, I'm least comfortable with the work of trying to apply Kovach's model without its explicitly Indigenous grounding. What Margaret Kovach has contributed was so clarifying for me as a teacher in the prison. But, I'm still me, I'm still a white woman who would not claim Indigenous ways of knowing. So I really wondered if Margaret Kovach's model could be used in a prison classroom if I'm the person that's doing the work. That is a really tough ethical question. Can you take a methodology that was put together by an Indigenous scholar and say, "Points two through five are going to be super helpful to the prison classroom"?

I absolutely stand by the claims that relationality was already there in the New Folsom classroom, that it needed to be recognized, and that the work of Indigenous scholars is very useful in thinking through that reality. So much amazing stuff has happened since we began thinking about what respect, reciprocity, and relationality look like in the AIC classroom at New Folsom. But that is the dilemma—when somebody like me comes in and says, "I think points two through five are applicable, but point number one is not something that is mine to claim, so I won't claim it." Is something essential lost? Can it be done? What's the most ethical thing to do here? And so that, for me, is the toughest question related to how the book played out.

STEVE: Kristin, to return to what you were saying at the outset: you don't disagree if people use some parts of your published work, but if they take that one story, you feel like that's different? There's a different set of criteria around use of certain material. How do you understand when people adopt an element of Indigenous scholarship and leave behind others? Is there a way to speak about that issue? Or is it so case specific to this project? Impossible?

KRISTIN: A little impossible. But I think that storytelling at least in my own communities is done with great intention. If an elder tells you a story, that story is being used in that moment to illuminate something for you and/or for the community. But that story can also be illuminating like twelve other things if told in a different context. So, when you're told a story, you need to question why that story, why to you, why in that context. And you might retell that story in a different context for different ends. And if we think of theory as story-as-theory, taking, as Anna says, Kovach's points two through five but leaving the rest can make good sense, because in that moment, in that space, in that context, that's the part of the story that's going to help you do the things that need to be done. And I think that is ethical, actually, so long as you are doing it for good reason with a good heart.

STEVE: My sense is that every book leaves questions that now need to be answered or work that now needs to be done. As you think about the work this book did, what sort of issues do you think it asks us to think more about? What would the next set of questions be? What types of work does this book still leave to be done?

ANNA: One issue that I think this book asks us to think further about is how to recognize relationality as foundational to strong methodologies that also forward rigorous educational work. I have many fears about putting anything in the public record, and one of them is that the book will be misconstrued in a way that authorizes the idea that instead of coming in and having one's teaching be grounded in some sort of disciplinary focus, that a misunderstood notion of relationality will lead folks to run classrooms that are nothing more than friendly jam sessions. That's absolutely not what the book is giving folks permission to do, but I do worry that in a context like prison, which is so dehumanizing, teachers will settle for spaces of friendship or connection instead of thinking critically and creatively about how to create respectful, reciprocal, and relational classrooms that still do their disciplinary work. I worry about this because I already know teachers who have fallen into the trap of thinking the *humanity* they bring is enough. And they never get around to teaching their craft.

I also worry that the claim about moving past an obsession with individual texts will end up obscuring incarcerated writers even further from the public. Obscurity for the individual is not a natural by-product of paying attention to relationality. Rather, the opposite should be true. But it would be the worst if we end up sort of making people more invisible as we try to revise our pedagogy.

So, for me, there are a couple of totally real dangers— people who decide they don't have to teach whatever they teach anymore—they're just going to hug and be nice. And then I worry about this idea of suppressing the voices of individual writers. Neither of those things should come out of the book, but those are the readers that worry me the most. So, circling back to your question of what's next: a context like prison is just so challenging to navigate bureaucratically and so exhausting for incarcerated students—and also, to a lesser degree, teachers. I think I would be afraid that somebody would take this book and think, "Oh good, we got that sorted. I'm using such-and-such methodology, so we're relational and respectful now. Prefect. I'm going to move on to the next thing."

I imagine that trying to figure out how to do this work well, and in this way, with the various challenges of local contexts, could take a while. I expect it might be my work for the next twenty years. And so, I worry that folks will bring Western ways of knowing and Western timetables to this book and be like, "Oh, cool. Good. Let's build on that." Whereas I was like, "I don't know. We're not good at this yet. It's just an idea. I'm trying, but I don't know." I would hate to see us rush on in this teleological way, to think we checked the "Respect" box and move on.

KRISTIN: I think this notion of "check the box, moving on" is really important for us to face as a field. As a reviewer I'm often asked, "Does this essay or book add a new perspective to the field?" But sometimes maybe it shouldn't. I think newness can erase stillness, the need to sit with things for a while. Yet it's hard to get published saying, "I'm doing a lot of walking along the river and thinking how to be better at this." Well, I could, but I'd have to generate some sort of walking theory, cite a bunch of embodiment scholarship, talk about examples in my teaching, when often it just needs to be, "I am thinking now. And I will be thinking for a while." But that's hard work as it's not the publishing and promotion economy we are a part of. And, so, to find ways to slow that down and to say like, "Hey, for the next twenty, thirty years, work on it, figure it out, take a lot of walks, sit and stare in the middle distance reflecting on your own culpability with colonialism." It's a hard space to be in for a lot of people for a number of reasons. It's hard to sit with something. To really sit with it and in it and figure that space out.

STEVE: I mean in some ways [Anna's] comment shows that deep community partnership won't produce a lot of scholarship because you're just resting there, dwelling there, learning there. And that doesn't necessarily produce that teleological look, and now there's a book—it's an opposition in a way. But that might be some of the impact of taking the theory seriously in the book. There's no next version of this book because the book led to deep partnership there for a long time, in a way.

KRISTIN: And I think if people really listen to what Anna's saying, I hope they would acknowledge that she's been sitting with it for a while, and even now her writing illustrates a sort of sitting with it. That type of relationality is slow and it's a process and if you're doing the work, you can't be running off to toot your own horn as it were.

STEVE: Yeah. Although I think academy is set up to toot your own horn. They basically hand you a horn and say, "Be really loud, maybe it'll get tenure." What gets lost sometimes, I think, is the ethics of the work. When we should broadcast our work, when we should hold it tight out of respect for our community, what we need to teach others about how to use the insights offered by a community. I think we are at a moment where there needs to be a redrawing of the ethics of use. New maps are required.

KRISTIN: Yeah. While I agree that folks of color can't take on all the burden of telling white people how to be better (white folks need to figure that out for themselves to a point), there's also a point at which we need to be respectful, I think, of our own cultural knowledge. And sometimes we need to directly tell people, "This knowledge is for you, this knowledge is not for you." Because unless they grew up with those protocols, they're not going to know. They likely grew up with wildly different protocols. A sharing and gifting community is radically different, and as tired as it can make me, I think we often just have to teach them if we expect anything better.

STEVE: I think that's what the best parts of the field are trying to figure out. Kristin, did you want to comment about the issue of use more broadly than perhaps in our earlier conversation?

KRISTIN: There's been a couple of moments I wanted to bring this story up. Last year I had a philosophy graduate student, Shelbi Nahwilet Meissner, in my American Indian Rhetorics class. She's Luiseño and wrote a piece on basket making as methodology. She comes from a basket-weaving people and family. When she presented her paper in class, she had a slide that essentially said, "Don't Cite This." She said, "This is my story, my methodology from my people and my land and my place. I'm sharing it with you to show you how I did this, but I'm not sharing it with you so that you can talk about basket-making methodology. Use your own methodologies, your own stories." That moment to me, and to the class, was really powerful, and I continue to be grateful for it. And I kind of wonder about the ways that we might do that in some of our own scholarship: "This is for you; this isn't for you."

ANNA: That is an amazing story. I just love the idea that
we need to be explicit about protocol in any culturally
and ideologically diverse scholarly community. I hope
that being explicit in these places leads to respect. When
somebody says, "Don't cite me," you don't. And I think
this really resonates with prison writing. I'm uncomfort-
able sometimes with the things that I see teachers publish
that they had heard in the prison class. In the context
of prison, you don't share other people's stories, because
there can be actual physical danger there. And even when
sharing information doesn't put someone in harm's way, it
can make their day-to-day life very difficult. Or be painful for the families of victims. For all these reasons, it's an
interesting place to kind of think through the ethics of
protocol for culturally and ideologically mixed company.

I really struggled with this as I was writing the book
because my most favorite stories and the most beautiful, the most powerful things I've seen happening in a
classroom, are 100 percent not in this book. And they
will never be in any book because it's just not appropriate.
They are not my stories and I don't have permission to
tell them. There were so many times I thought, "Oh, you
know what would really illustrate that point well?" And
then I would say to myself, "Nope. That's not my story.
That one's not mine either. Nope. Not that one either."

I think that is why I ended up trying to write some of
the narrative pieces from my own perspective as a teacher
because that's the only thing that's actually safe for me to
write, and to do anything else is just so fundamentally
disrespectful to the folks that come to class. And so I just
really appreciate what your student did in the classroom,
and I would love to see us do more of that for each other.

STEVE: It's an interesting way to frame the book, to say,
"Well, read it for what's in there with the recognition that
I also intentionally left some stories/theories out." The

silences are as important as when you voice things. And I think it's an interesting project then to say, "I consciously chose silence as an ethical stance." I think that's an interesting way to understand partially how you approached this book and how you thought it through with Kristin.

As we finish up, I want to ask about a silence in the book not chosen by you. The absence of Marty and Spoon. One of the difficulties you had in writing this book was that Marty and Spoon's participation ends. I wondered how you thought the book was impacted by them, for all the reasons you say in the book, not really being able to take part in the writing and revision of the manuscript. How did that impact the work, do you think? I'm also thinking that your original motivation for the book was to share their pedagogical vision and practices with the field. I am hoping you can let the readers hear a bit of what you think they might have (or did) bring to this project.

ANNA: So again, this is tricky, right? Because Spoon and Marty were transferred, and I really have not had a chance to talk with them. So I can't speak for them here. I don't know if they would like this book. I can imagine some of their critiques, and I am smiling here, because I am pretty sure they would focus on different parts of the text and maybe even have conflicting opinions about what it could have or should have accomplished. With that said, I think Spoon's and Marty's contributions to the narrative of the book show up toward the front because their contributions to the history and culture of Arts in Corrections at New Folsom were profound. They made something strong and beautiful out of a cinderblock room, and their presence was felt for a long time after they were gone. I actually still feel like the room belongs to their spirits. I sometimes forget, when I am there, that they are not.

As I share in the book, I was sort of coming in as they were going out, and I'm really grateful for the overlap. They said a lot of things that set me on a good path and some of them are in the book. Here I am thinking of Marty's refrain about not trying to fix or save people. So I really heard that point. I'm appreciative of that wisdom and I think that comes out in the book.

I think Spoon's contribution to the book are different. What I love about his contribution is that he has published more. So I really enjoy interacting with Spoon in the same way I interact with any other scholar whose work I read. I appreciate that he has gone to the trouble, as I can imagine that it's a lot of work to try to enter the public record and produce scholarship while you're incarcerated.

So my interactions with those two folks when I knew them, and since then, are really different. Those two teachers set me on a path, got me going, established me in that space. But the people whose work is published in the book and the stories that are told in the book are mostly from folks that I have worked with more recently. And so most of the relational work of the book is really not with either Spoon or Marty, which explains why they become more and more absent as the book goes on. If you're doing relational work, then it has to be with people that you're actually in relationship with. I really don't know what Spoon and Marty would say about this book, but I hope that no matter their opinions about it, that they would recognize that their legacy at New Folsom is still growing—that their relationship with the space and the people in it is a living, breathing thing.

## NOTES

### Foreword

1. *Anishinaabekwe* means "Anishinaabe women." The Anishinaabe are a group of Indigenous peoples from the Great Lakes region of North America and include the Ojibwe, of which I am a part. I am also ethnically and culturally Finnish.

### 1. Getting Inside

1. See Deloria, *Spirit*; Cordova; Maracle; Hampton; Mihesuah and Wilson; S. Wilson; Smith; Haas, "Toward"; Arola, "Slow Composition"; King, Gubele, and Anderson.
2. From here on, I refer to my dad by his last name. Despite the concern that referring to him in the third person erases the familial connection, I believe it is important for his name to be recognized when talking about his work.
3. The Prison Arts Project was funded by the California Arts Council, the National Endowment for the Arts, the San Francisco Foundation, and the Law Enforcement Assistance Administration.
4. Information about Arts in Corrections is available in the UCLA archive, "Arts-in-Corrections Records," and in the following publications: Bernstein; Brewster, "California," *Evaluation*; P. Brown; Cleveland, *Art*, "California's Arts-in-Correction," "Common Sense"; Lockard and Rankins-Robertson; Tannenbaum; Tannenbaum and Jackson; Wenzer.
5. As a new PhD student, my scope of understanding was (of course) limited, but I think the story is worth telling because I feel confident my early reading lists are representative of many new graduate students. The disequilibrium I was feeling at the time informs my desire to see the field invite a wider range of scholars and ideas onto early program reading lists and class offerings.
6. M. Alexander; W. Alexander; A. Davis, *Abolition*; Gilmore; Hartnett; Mauer; Meiners, *Right*; Parenti; Rusche and Kirchheimer.

7. Braman; A. Davis, *Are Prisons*; Forman; Herivel and Wright; Lawston and Lucas; Mauer and Chesney-Lind; Pager; Patton; Stevenson.

## 2. The Process of Re-Membering

1. Scholars Flower invokes include Anzaldúa; Cushman, "Opinion"; Deans; Hauser and Grim; Roberts-Miller; Shor and Pari; Weisser.
2. See Billington; Brewster, "California"; Coe; Halperin et al.; Hartman, *Mother*; Masters; Pompa, "Breaking Down," "Service-Learning"; Shailor; Tannenbaum and Jackson.
3. The reference to meaning-making here draws on the work of Ann Berthoff, Sharon Crowley, Susanne Langer, Jasper Neel, and Raúl Sanchez.
4. The oratorio was written and arranged by Marty Williams.

## 3. Toward Relational Methodologies

1. The prison ecosystem is complex, inherently dangerous, and retaliatory. Broadcasting information about a person's crime, gang affiliation, or location can put both them and their families in physical danger. Sharing information about incarcerated students' thoughts or feelings might make them seem weak and change the precarious balance of power for them in their cellblock or interior social networks. Respect for the rights and privacy of victims adds an additional layer of complexity to the circulation of information gleaned from the prison classroom.
2. Arola, "It's My Revolution," "Slow Composition"; Arola and Arola; Cushman, "Decolonizing," "Translingual," "Wampum"; Frost; Haas, "Wampum"; King, Gubele, and Anderson; and Powell, "2012 CCCC," to name a few.
3. Here I am thinking of both space and place theory broadly (Lefebvre; Soja; Tuan) and spatial rhetorics more specifically (Mauk; Mountford; Payne; and Reynolds, to name a few).
4. The CDCR has strict rules in place to prevent overfamiliarity by explicitly forbidding staff, contractors, and volunteers from having any contact with inmates or their families outside of class. Like the constraining structures of the IRB, the official CDCR prohibitions against overfamiliarity are neither conspiratorial nor outrageous. Yet teachers *can* foster deeply meaningful relationships in the classroom that still meet the standards of the institution and do not jeopardize the classroom by bringing it under the scrutiny of administrative hyper-observation. Teachers who patiently learn the

rules and follow them may even find allies in the prison bureaucracy that can help them sustain their program and might even sanction relationships that appear, on first look, to be a breach of overfamiliarity. This has been the case with my relationship with Carol Hinds.

### 4. Opportunities and Options

1. The FA program curriculum includes twenty-four lessons. At a rate of one exchange per month, it would take a participant a minimum of two years to work through the curriculum with their partner.

## BIBLIOGRAPHY

Alexander, Michelle. *The New Jim Crow: Mass Incarceration in the Age of Colorblindness*. The New Press, 2010.

Alexander, William. *Is William Martinez Not Our Brother? Twenty Years of the Prison Creative Arts Project*. U of Michigan P, 2010.

Anzaldúa, Gloria. *Borderlands/La Frontera: The New Mestiza*. Aunt Lute Books, 1987.

Arola, Kristin L. "It's My Revolution: Learning to See the Mixedblood." *Composing(media) = Composing(embodiment): Bodies, Technologies, Writing, the Teaching of Writing*, edited by Kristin L. Arola and Anne Frances Wysocki, Utah State UP, 2012, pp. 213–38.

———. "Slow Composition: An Indigenous Approach to Digital Making." Digital Discussions in the Humanities and Social Sciences Colloquia Series, 2014, Virginia Polytechnic Institute and State University, Blacksburg, VA.

Arola, Kristin L., and Adam Arola. "An Ethics of Assemblage: Creative Repetition and the 'Electric Pow Wow.'" *Assembling Composition*, edited by Kathleen Blake Yancy and Stephen McElroy, Conference on College Composition and Communication, 2017, pp. 204–21.

Arrighi, Giovanni. *The Long Twentieth Century: Money, Power, and the Origins of our Times*. Verso, 2010.

Arts-in-Corrections Records. University of California, Los Angeles, Archives, Record Series 721.

Atkinson, Judy. "Privileging Indigenous Research Methodologies." Indigenous Voices Conference, 2001, Cairns.

Baldwin, James. "In Search of a Majority." *Nobody Knows My Name*. Dial Press, 1961.

Bernstein, Lee. *America Is the Prison: Arts and Politics in Prison in The 1970s*. The U of North Carolina P, 2010.

Berthoff, Ann E. "Is Teaching Still Possible? Writing, Meaning, and Higher Order Reasoning." *Cross-Talk in Comp Theory*, edited by Victor Villanueva, 2nd ed., National Council of Teachers of English, 2003, pp. 329–43.

———. "Learning the Uses of Chaos." Paper presented at the Annual Meeting of the Canadian Council of Teachers of English, Ottawa, Canada, May 1979.

———. *The Making of Meaning: Metaphors, Models, and Maxims for Writing Teachers.* Boynton/Cook, 1981.

———. "Response to Janice Lauer, 'Counterstatement.'" *College Composition and Communication*, vol. 23, no. 5, 1972, pp. 414–16.

Biko, Steve. *I Write What I Like.* San Francisco: Harper & Row, 1978.

Billington, Josie. "'Reading for Life': Prison Reading Groups in Practice and Theory." *Critical Survey*, vol. 23, no. 3, 2011, pp. 67–85.

Blackburn, Lorelei, and Ellen Cushman. "Assessing Sustainability: The Class That Went Terribly Wrong." *Unsustainable: Re-Imagining Community Literacy, Public Writing, Service–Learning and the University*, edited by Jessica Restaino and Laurie JC Cella, Lexington Books, 2013, pp. 161–78.

Bosworth, Mary. *Engendering Resistance: Agency and Power in Women's Prisons.* Ashgate/Dartmouth, 1999.

Braman, Donald. "Families and Incarceration." *Invisible Punishment: The Collateral Consequences of Mass Imprisonment*, edited by Mauer, Marc, and Meda Chesney-Lind, The New Press, 2002.

Branch, Kirk. *"Eyes on the Ought to Be": What We Teach About When We Teach About Literacy.* Hampton Press, 2007.

Brandt, Deborah. *Literacy in American Lives.* Cambridge UP, 2001.

Brewster, Larry, and Peter Merts. *Paths of Discovery: Art Practice and Its Impact in California Prisons.* 2nd ed., CreateSpace Independent Publishing Platform, 2015.

Brewster, Lawrence G. "The California Arts-in-Corrections Music Programme: A Qualitative Study." *International Journal of Community Music*, vol. 3, no. 1, 2010, pp. 33–46.

———. *An Evaluation of the Arts-in-Corrections Program of the California Department of Corrections.* Prepared for William James Association, 1983, http://www.williamjamesassociation.org/reports/Brewster_report_full.pdf. Accessed 12 Sept. 2013.

Brodkey, Linda. "On the Subjects of Class and Gender in 'The Literacy Letters.'" *Cross-Talk in Comp Theory*, edited by Victor Villanueva, 2nd ed., National Council of Teachers of English, 2003, pp. 677–96.

Brown, Patricia Leigh. "No License Plates Here: Using Art to Transcend Prison Walls." *New York Times*, 2 Apr. 2017.

Brown, Wendy. *Undoing the Demos: Neoliberalism's Stealth Revolution.* Zone Books, 2015.

Burke, Kenneth. *Language as Symbolic Action: Essays on Life, Literature, and Method.* U of California P, 1966.

Burkhart, Brian Yazzie. "What Coyote and Thales Can Teach Us: An Outline of American Indian Epistemology." *American Indian Thought,* edited by Anne Waters, Blackwell, 2004, pp. 15–26.

Bury, J. B. *The Idea of Progress: An Inquiry into Its Origin and Growth.* Dover, 1932.

Cajete, Gregory. "A Philosophy of Native Science." *American Indian Thought,* edited by Anne Waters, Blackwell Publishing, 2004, pp. 45–57.

California Rehabilitation Oversight Board. *California Rehabilitation Oversight Board: September 15, 2013 Biannual Report,* 11 Oct. 2013, https://www.crob.ca.gov//media/crob/reports/C-ROB_Biannual_Report_September_15_2013.pdf.

Carlson, Jim. "MEMORANDUM to Facility Captain." Arts-in-Corrections Record, Record Series 721, 2007. University of California, Los Angeles, Archives.

Carnes, Aaron. "Jailhouse Blues: Henry Robinett on Teaching Inmates to Play the Guitar." *The Sun Interview,* October 2017.

Castro, Erin L., and Michael Brawn. "Critiquing Critical Pedagogies Inside the Prison Classroom: A Dialogue Between Student and Teacher." *Harvard Educational Review,* vol. 87, no. 1, 2017, pp. 99–121.

Chilisa, Bagele. *Indigenous Research Methodologies.* Thousand Oaks, SAGE, 2012.

Cleveland, William. *Art in Other Places: Artists at Work in America's Community and Social Institutions.* Praeger Publishers, 2000.

———. "California's Arts-in-Corrections: Discipline, Imagination, and Opportunity." *Higher Education in Prison: A Contradiction in Terms?,* edited by Miriam Williford, Oryx Press, 1994.

———. "Common Sense and Common Ground: Survival Skills for Artists Working in Correctional Institutions." *Teaching the Arts behind Bars,* Northeastern UP, 2003, pp. 28–39.

Coe, Kirsten K. "Ecology behind Bars: A Teaching Garden Cultivates Free Minds." *The Radical Teacher,* vol. 95, 2013, pp. 56–60.

Cohen, Stanley, and Laurie Taylor. *Psychological Survival: The Experience of Long-Term Imprisonment.* Pantheon Books, 1972.

Condon, Frankie. *I Hope I Join the Band: Narrative, Affiliation, and Antiracist Rhetoric.* Utah State UP, 2012.

Cordova, V. F. *How It Is: The Native American Philosophy of V. F. Cordova,* edited by Kathleen Dean Moore, et al., U of Arizona P, 2007.

Crowley, Sharon. "Of Gorgias and Grammatology." *College Composition and Communication,* vol. 30, no. 3, 1979, pp. 279–84.

———. *A Teacher's Introduction to Deconstruction.* National Council of Teachers of English, 1989.

Cummins, Eric. *The Rise and Fall of California's Radical Prison Movement.* Stanford UP, 1994.

Cushman, Ellen. "Decolonizing Validity." *Journal of Writing Assessment,* vol. 9, no. 1, 2016.

———, et al., editors. *Literacy: A Critical Sourcebook.* Bedford/St. Martin's, 2001.

———. "Opinion: The Public Intellectual, Service Learning, and Activist Research." *College English,* vol. 61, no. 3, 1999, pp. 328–36.

———. "Translingual and Decolonial Approaches to Meaning Making." *College English,* vol. 78, no. 3, 2016, pp. 234–42.

———. "Wampum, Sequoyan, and Story: Decolonizing the Digital Archive." *College English,* vol. 76, no. 2, 2013, pp. 115–135.

Cushman, Ellen, and Shreelina Ghosh. "The Mediation of Cultural Memory: Digital Preservation in the Cases of Classical Indian Dance and the Cherokee Stomp Dance." *The Journal of Popular Culture,* vol. 45, no. 2, 2012, pp. 264–83.

Daly, Mary. *Amazon Grace: Re-Calling the Courage to Sin Big.* New York: Palgrave Macmillan, 2006.

Davis, Angela Y. *Abolition Democracy: Beyond Empire, Prisons, and Torture.* Seven Stories Press, 2005.

———. *Are Prisons Obsolete?* Seven Stories Press, 2003.

———. *Freedom Is a Constant Struggle: Ferguson, Palestine, and the Foundations of a Movement,* edited by Frank Barat. Haymarket Books, 2016.

Davis, Lois M., et al. *How Effective is Correctional Education, and Where Do We Go From Here? The Results of a Comprehensive Evaluation.* RAND Corporation, 2014.

Deans, Thomas. *Writing Partnerships: Service-Learning in Composition.* National Council of Teachers of English, 2000.

de Certeau, Michel. *The Practice of Everyday Life.* U of California P, 2002.

Deloria, Vine Jr. "Philosophy and the Tribal Peoples." *American Indian Thought,* edited by Anne Waters, Blackwell, 2004, pp. 3–11.

———. *Spirit and Reason: The Vine Deloria, Jr., Reader,* edited by Barbara Deloria, Kristen Foehner, and Sam Scinta, Fulcrum, 1999.

Derrida, Jacques. *Of Grammatology*. Translated by Gayatri Chakravorty Spivak, corrected ed., John Hopkins UP, 1997.

———. *Of Spirit: Heidegger and the Question*. Translated by Geoffrey Bennington and Rachel Bowlby, U of Chicago P, 1989.

———. "Otobiographies: The Teaching of Nietzsche and the Politics of the Proper Name." *The Ear of the Other: Otobiography, Transference, Translation*. Translated by Avital Ronell, Schocken Books, 1985, pp. 3–38.

De Veaux, Alexis. *Warrior Poet: A Biography of Audre Lorde*. New York: W. W. Norton, 2004.

Douglass, Frederick, John W. Blassingame, and John R. McKivigan. *The Frederick Douglass Papers. Series One*. Yale UP, 1979.

Downes, David, and Paul Rock. *Understanding Deviance: A Guide to the Sociology of Crime and Rule-Breaking*. 2nd ed., Clarendon Press, 1988.

Drabinski, Kate, and Gillian Harkins. "Introduction: Teaching Inside Carceral Institutions." *Radical Teacher*, no. 95, 2012, pp. 3–9.

Drum, Kevin. "A Very Brief History of Super-Predators." *Mother Jones*. March 3, 2016.

Duguid, Stephen. "Subjects and Objects in Modern Corrections." *Journal of Correctional Education*, vol. 51, no. 2, 2000, pp. 241–55.

DuVernay, Ava, director and producer. *13th*. Forward Movement/Kandoo Films, 2016.

Ensler, Eve. *What I Want My Words to Do to You: Voices from Inside a Women's Maximum Security Prison*. Borrowed Light: PBS Home Video, 2003.

Feigenbaum, Paul, Sharayna Douglas, and Maria Lovett. "Tales from the Crawl Space: Asserting Youth Agency within an Unsustainable Education System." *Unsustainable: Re-Imagining Community Literacy, Public Writing, Service–Learning and the University*, edited by Jessica Restaino and Laurie JC Cella, Lexington Books, 2013, pp. 33–54.

Flower, Linda. *Community Literacy and the Rhetoric of Public Engagement*. Southern Illinois UP, 2008.

Forman, Jr., James. "Children, Cops, and Citizenship: Why Conservatives Should Oppose Racial Profiling." *Invisible Punishment: The Collateral Consequences of Mass Imprisonment*, edited by Marc Mauer and Meda Chesney-Lind, New Press, 2002.

Frost, Alanna. "Literacy Stewardship: Dakelh Women Composing Culture." *College Composition and Communication*, vol. 63, no. 1, 2011, pp. 54–74.

Gilmore, Ruth Wilson. *Golden Gulag: Prisons, Surplus, Crisis, and Opposition in Globalizing California.* U of California P, 2007.

Gilyard, Keith. *Liberation Memories: The Rhetoric and Poetics of John Oliver Killens.* Wayne State UP, 2003.

Goldblatt, Eli. *Because We Live Here: Sponsoring Literacy beyond the College Curriculum.* Hampton Press, 2007.

Goldstein, Joseph. "Pregnant Inmates Say a Federal Jail Is No Place for Them, and Some Judges Agree." *New York Times,* 12 March 2017.

Gottschalk, Marie. *Caught: The Prison State and the Lockdown of American Politics.* Princeton UP, 2015.

Grabill, Jeffrey T. *Community Literacy Programs and the Politics of Change.* State U of New York P, 2001.

Gramsci, Antonio. *Selections from the Prison Notebooks.* Edited by Quintin Hoare and Geoffrey Nowell Smith, International Publishers, 1971.

Grosfoguel, Ramón. "Colonial Difference, Geopolitics of Knowledge, and Global Coloniality in the Modern/Colonial Capitalist World-System." *Review,* vol. 25, no. 3, 2002, pp. 203–24.

Guest, Sara, Hanna Neuschwander, and Robyn Steely. "Respect, Writing, Community: Write around Portland." *Circulating Communities: The Tactics and Strategies of Community Publishing,* edited by Paula Mathieu, Steve Parks, and Tiffany Rousculp, Lexington Books, 2012.

Haas, Angela M. "Race, Rhetoric, and Technology: A Case Study of Decolonial Technical Communication Theory, Methodology, and Pedagogy." *Journal of Business and Technical Communication,* vol. 26, no. 3, 2012, pp. 277–310.

———. "Toward a Decolonial Digital and Visual American Indian Rhetorics Pedagogy." *Survivance, Sovereignty, and Story: Teaching American Indian Rhetorics,* edited by Lisa King, Rose Gubele, and Joyce Rain Anderson, Utah State UP, 2015, pp. 188–208.

———. "Wampum as Hypertext: An American Indian Intellectual Tradition of Multimedia Theory and Practice." *Studies in American Indian Literatures,* vol. 19, no. 4, 2007, pp. 77–100.

Halperin, Ronnie, Suzanne Kessler, and Dana Braunschweiger. "Rehabilitation through the Arts: Impact on Participants' Engagement in Educational Programs." *The Journal of Correctional Education,* vol. 63, no. 1, 2012, pp. 6–23.

Hampton, Eber. "Memory Comes before Knowledge: Research May Improve If Researchers Remember Their Motives." *Canadian Journal of Native Education,* vol. 21, 1995 pp. 46–54.

Harkinson, Josh. "It's 2017, and Most States Still Allow Shacking of Prisoners during Labor and Delivery." *Mother Jones,* 5 Aug. 2017.

Hartman, Kenneth E. *Mother California: A Story of Redemption Behind Bars*. New York: Atlas, 2009.

———, editor. *Too Cruel, Not Unusual Enough*. The Other Death Penalty Project, 2013.

Hartnett, Stephen John, editor. *Challenging the Prison-Industrial Complex: Activism, Arts, and Educational Alternatives*. U of Illinois P, 2010.

Haslam, Jason. "The State of Prison." *American Quarterly*, vol. 60, no. 2, 2008, pp. 467–79.

Hassine, Victor. *Life without Parole: Living in Prison Today*. Roxburg, 1999.

Hauser, Gerard A., and Amy Grim, editors. *Rhetorical Democracy: Discursive Practices of Civic Engagement*. Erlbaum, 2004.

Herivel, Tara, and Paul Wright, editors. *Prison Nation: The Warehousing of America's Poor*. Routledge, 2003.

Hogan, Linda. "Forward: Viola Cordova, Perspectives by Linda Hogan." *How It Is: The Native American Philosophy of V. F. Cordova*, edited by Kathleen Dean Moore et al., U of Arizona P, 2007.

hooks, bell. *Teaching to Transgress: Education as the Practice of Freedom*. Routledge, 1994.

Horton, Myles, and Paulo Freire. *We Make the Road by Walking: Conversations on Education and Social Change*, edited by Brenda Bell, John Gaventa, and John Peters, Temple UP, 1990.

Howe, LeAnne. "The Story of America: A Tribalography." *Clearing a Path: Theorizing the Past in Native American Studies*, edited by Nancy Shoemaker, Routledge, 2002, pp. 29–48.

Hunter, Ian. *Rethinking the School: Subjectivity, Bureaucracy, Criticism*. St. Martin's Press, 1994.

Hyde, Lewis. *Trickster Makes This World: Mischief, Myth, and Art*. Farrar, Straus and Giroux, 2010.

Inoue, Asao B. *Antiracist Writing Assessment Ecologies: Teaching and Assessing Writing for a Socially Just Future*. WAC Clearinghouse, 2015.

———. "How Do We Language So People Stop Killing Each Other, or What Do We Do about White Language Supremacy?" Keynote Address, CCCC Annual Convention, Pittsburgh, PA, 14 Mar. 2019, https://www.youtube.com/watch?v=brPGTewcDYY

Jackson, Spoon. "Go On." *Too Cruel, Not Unusual Enough*, edited by Kenneth E. Hartman, The Other Death Penalty Project, 2013, pp. 23–28.

———. *Nowhere but Barstow and Prison*. Pen America, 24 June 2008, pen.org/nowhere-but-barstow-and-prison/.

———. "Speaking in Poems." *Teaching Artist Journal*, vol. 5, no. 1, 2007, pp. 22–26.

Jacobi, Tobi. "Curating Counternarratives beyond Bars; Speaking Out with Writers at a County Jail." *Prison Pedagogies: Learning and Teaching with Imprisoned Writers*, edited by Joe Lockhard and Sherry Rankins-Robertson, Syracuse UP, 2018, pp. 109–26.

———. "Speaking Out for Social Justice: The Problems and Possibilities of US Women's Prison and Jail Writing Workshops." *Critical Survey*, vol. 23, no. 3, 2011, pp. 40–54.

Jacobi, Tobi, and Stephanie L. Becker. "Rewriting Confinement: Feminist and Queer Critical Literacy in SpeakOut! Writing Workshops." *Radical Teacher*, no. 95, 2013, pp. 32–40.

Jones, Kalinda, Anthony Ferguson, Christian Ramirez, and Michael Owens. "Seen but Not Heard: Personal Narratives of Systemic Failure within the School-to-Prison Pipeline." *Taboo: The Journal of Culture and Education*, vol. 17, no. 4, 2018, pp. 49–68.

Kahan, Paul. *Seminary of Virtue: The Ideology and Practice of Inmate Reform at Eastern State Penitentiary, 1829–1971*. Peter Lang, 2012.

Karpowitz, Daniel. *College in Prison: Reading in an Age of Mass Incarceration*. Rutgers UP, 2017.

Katz, Steven B. "The Ethic of Expediency: Classical Rhetoric, Technology, and the Holocaust." *College English*, vol. 54, no. 3, 1992, pp. 255–75.

Kerschbaum, Stephanie L. *Toward a New Rhetoric of Difference*. Conference on College Composition and Communication/National Council of Teachers of English, 2014.

Kilgore, James. "Is Another Pedagogical World Possible? Teaching Globalization to My Fellow Prisoners." *Radical Teacher*, no. 95, 2013, pp. 40–51.

King, Lisa, Rose Gubele, and Joyce Rain Anderson, editors. *Survivance, Sovereignty, and Story: Teaching American Indian Rhetorics*. Utah State UP, 2015.

Kovach, Margaret. *Indigenous Methodologies: Characteristics, Conversations, and Contexts*. U of Toronto P, 2009.

Langer, Susanne K. *Philosophy in a New Key: A Study in the Symbolism of Reason, Rite, and Art*. 2nd ed., The New American Library, 1942.

Latour, Bruno. *Aramis, or, the Love of Technology*. Translated by Catherine Porter, Harvard UP, 1996.

———. *We Have Never Been Modern*. Translated by Catherine Porter, Harvard UP, 1993.

Lauer, Janice. "Response to Ann E. Berthoff, 'The Problem of Problem Solving.'" *College Composition and Communication*, vol. 23, no. 2, 1972, pp. 208–10.

Lawston, Jodie Michelle, and Ashley E. Lucas. *Razor Wire Women: Prisoners, Activists, Scholars, and Artists.* State U of New York Press, 2011.

Lefebvre, Henri. *The Production of Space.* Translated by Donald Nicholson-Smith, Blackwell, 1991.

Lemke, Jay. *Textual Politics: Discourse and Social Dynamics.* Taylor & Francis, 1995.

Lockard, Joe. "Prison Writing Education and US Working-Class Consciousness." *Prison Pedagogies,* edited by Joe Lockard and Sherry Rankins-Robertson, Syracuse UP, 2018, pp. 11–31.

Lockard, Joe, and Sherry Rankins-Robertson. "The Right to Education, Prison-University Partnerships, and Online Writing Pedagogy in the US." *Critical Survey,* vol. 23, no. 3, 2011, pp. 23–39.

Lorde, Audre. "The Master's Tools Will Never Dismantle the Master's House." *Sister Outsider: Essays and Speeches.* Crossing Press, 1984, pp. 110–14.

Maracle, Lee. *Oratory: Coming to Theory.* North Vancouver: Gallerie Publications, 1990.

Martinson, Robert. "California Research at the Crossroads." *Crime and Delinquency,* vol. 22, no. 2, 1976, pp. 180–91.

———. "What Works? Questions and Answers about Prison Reform." *The Public Interest,* 1974, pp. 22–54.

Masters, Jarvis Jay. *That Bird Has My Wings: The Autobiography of an Innocent Man on Death Row.* HarperOne, 2009.

Mathieu, Paula. "After Tactics, What Comes Next?" *Unsustainable: Re-Imagining Community Literacy, Public Writing, Service–Learning and the University,* edited by Jessica Restaino and Laurie JC Cella, Lexington Books, 2013, pp. 17–32.

———. *Tactics of Hope: The Public Turn in English Composition.* Boynton/Cook, 2005.

Mathieu, Paula, Steve Parks, and Tiffany Rousculp, editors. *Circulating Communities: The Tactics and Strategies of Community Publishing.* Lexington Books, 2012.

Mauer, Marc. *Race to Incarcerate.* The New Press, 1999.

Mauer, Marc, and Meda Chesney-Lind, editors. *Invisible Punishment: The Collateral Consequences of Mass Imprisonment.* The New Press, 2002.

Mauk, Johnathon. "Location, Location, Location: The 'Real' (E)states of Being, Writing, and Thinking in Composition." *College English,* vol. 65, no. 4, 2003, pp. 368–88.

Meiners, Erica R. "Ending the School-to-Prison Pipeline/Building Abolition Futures." *Urban Review,* vol. 43, no. 4, 2011, pp. 547-65.

———. *Right to Be Hostile: Schools, Prisons, and the Making of Public Enemies*. Routledge, 2007.

Mignolo, Walter D. *The Darker Side of Western Modernity: Global Futures, Decolonial Options*. Duke UP, 2011.

Mihesuah, Devon Abbott, and Angela Cavender Wilson, editors. *Indigenizing the Academy: Transforming Scholarship and Empowering Communities*. U of Nebraska P, 2004.

Miller, Richard E. *As If Learning Mattered: Reforming Higher Education*. Cornell UP, 1998.

Mills, Charles W. *The Racial Contract*. Cornell UP, 1999.

Momaday, N. Scott. *The Man Made of Words: Essays, Stories, Passages*. St. Martin's Press, 1997.

Mountford, Roxanne. "On Gender and Rhetorical Space." *Rhetorical Society Quarterly*, vol. 31, no. 1, 2001, pp. 41–71.

Muhammad, Bahiyyah, and Muntaquim Muhammad. *The Prison Alphabet: An Educational Picture Book for Children of Incarcerated Parents*. Goldest Karat, 2014.

Ndlovu-Gatsheni, Sabelo J., and Siphamandla Zondi. *Decolonizing the University, Knowledge Systems and Disciplines in Africa*. Carolina Academic Press, 2016.

Neel, Jasper. *Plato, Derrida, and Writing*. Southern Illinois UP, 1988.

Ngũgĩ wa Thiong'o. *Re-membering Africa*. Kampala, East African Educational Publishers, 2009.

Novek, Eleanor M., and Rebecca Sanford. "Our Silences Will Hurt Us: Journalistic Writing in a Women's Prison." *Why We Write: The Politics and Practice of Writing for Social Change*, edited by Jim Downs, Routledge, 2006, pp. 111–23.

Owens, Louis. *Mixedblood Messages: Literature, Film, Family, Place*. U of Oklahoma P, 1998.

———. *Other Destinies: Understanding the American Indian Novel*. U of Oklahoma P, 1992.

Pager, Devah. *Marked: Race, Crime, and Finding Work in an Era of Mass Incarceration*. U of Chicago P, 2007.

Parenti, Christian. *Lockdown America: Police and Prisons in the Age of Crisis*. Verso, 2000.

Patton, Charles III. "Incarceration Data: Selected Comparisons." *Race/Ethnicity: Multidisciplinary Global Contexts*, vol. 2, no. 1, 2008, pp. 151–56.

Payne, Darin. "English Studies in Levittown: Rhetorics of Space and Technology in Course-Management Software." *College English*, vol. 67, no. 5, 2005, pp. 483–507.

Plemons, Anna. "Beyond Progress: Indigenous Scholars, Relational Methodologies, and Decolonial Options for the Prison Classroom." *Critical Perspectives on Teaching in Prison: Students and Instructors on Pedagogy behind the Wall,* edited by Rebecca Ginsburg, Routledge, 2019, pp. 80–91.

———. "Literacy as an Act of Creative Resistance: Joining the Work of Incarcerated Teaching Artists at a Maximum-Security Prison." *Community Literacy Journal,* vol. 7, no. 2, 2013, pp. 39–52.

———. "Saying Good-Bye, Keeping My Keys." *Teaching Artist Journal,* vol. 11, no. 2, 2013, pp. 97–104.

———. "Something Other Than Progress: Indigenous Methodologies and Higher Education in Prison." *Prison Pedagogies: Learning and Teaching with Imprisoned Writers,* edited by Joe Lockard and Sherry Rankins-Robertson, Syracuse UP, 2018, pp. 88–108.

Pompa, Lori. "Breaking Down the Walls: Inside-Out Learning and the Pedagogy of Transformation." *Challenging the Prison-Industrial Complex: Activism, Arts, and Educational Alternatives,* edited by Stephen J. Hartnett, U of Illinois P, 2011, pp. 253–72.

———. "Service-Learning as Crucible: Reflections on Immersion, Context, Power, and Transformation." *Michigan Journal of Community Service Learning,* vol. 9, no. 1, 2002, pp. 67–76.

Powell, Malea. "2012 CCCC Chair's Address: Stories Take Place: A Performance in One Act." *College Composition and Communication,* vol. 64, no. 2, 2012, pp. 383–406.

———. "Blood and Scholarship: One Mixed-Blood's Story." *Race, Rhetoric, and Composition,* edited by Keith Gilyard, Boynton/Cook, 1999, pp. 1–16.

———. "Down by the River, or How Susan La Flesche Picotte Can Teach Us about Alliance as a Practice of Survivance." *College English,* vol. 67, no. 1, 2004, pp. 38–60.

———. "Rhetorics of Survivance: How American Indians Use Writing." *College Composition and Communication,* vol. 53, no. 3, 2002, pp. 396–434.

Rafay, Atif. "An 'Impossible Profession'? The Radical University in Prison." *Radical Teacher,* vol. 95, 2013, pp. 10–21.

Ratcliffe, Krista. *Rhetorical Listening: Identification, Gender, Whiteness.* Southern Illinois UP, 2005.

Restaino, Jessica, and Laurie JC Cella, editors. *Unsustainable: Re-imagining Community Literacy, Public Writing, Service-Learning and the University.* Lexington Books, 2013.

Reynolds, Nedra. *Geographies of Writing: Inhabiting Places and Encountering Differences*. Southern Illinois UP, 2004.

Rich, Adrienne. *Blood, Bread, and Poetry: Selected Prose, 1979–1985*. Norton, 1986.

Roberts-Miller, Patricia. *Deliberate Conflict: Argument, Political Theory, and Composition Classes*. Southern Illinois UP, 2004.

Rodríguez, Dylan. "The Disorientation of the Teaching Act: Abolition as Pedagogical Position." *Radical Teacher*, vol. 88, 2010, pp. 7–19.

Rolston, Simon. "Conversion and the Story of the American Prison." *Critical Survey*, vol. 23, no. 3, 2011, pp. 103–18.

Rousculp, Tiffany. *Rhetoric of Respect: Recognizing Change at a Community Writing Center*. National Council of Teachers of English, 2014.

Rusche, Georg, and Otto Kirchheimer. *Punishment and Social Structure*. Transaction Publishers, 2003.

Sánchez, Raúl. *The Function of Theory in Composition Studies*. State U of New York P, 2006.

Sanders, Mark. *Complicities: The Intellectual and Apartheid*. Duke UP, 2002.

Santos, Boaventura de Sousa. "Beyond Abyssal Thinking: From Global Lines to Ecologies of Knowledges." *Review XXX.1*, 2007, pp. 45–89.

Scott, Robert. "Distinguishing Radical Teaching from Merely Having Intense Experiences While Teaching in Prison." *Radical Teacher*, no. 95, 2013, pp. 22–32.

———. "Using Critical Pedagogy to Connect Prison Education and Prison Abolitionism." *Saint Louis University Public Law Review*, vol. 33, no. 2, 2014, pp. 401–14.

Shafer, Gregory. "Composition and a Prison Community of Writers." *English Journal*, vol. 90, no. 5, 2001, pp. 75–81.

Shailor, Jonathan. *Performing New Lives: Prison Theatre*. Jessica Kingsley Publishers, 2010.

Shor, Ira, and Carolina Pari, editors. *Critical Literacy in Action: Writing Words, Changing Worlds*. Boynton/Cook, 1999.

Smith, Linda Tuhiwai. *Decolonizing Methodologies: Research and Indigenous Peoples*. 2nd ed., Zed Books, 2012.

Soja, Edward W. *Postmodern Geographies: The Reassertion of Space in Critical Social Theory*. Verso, 1989.

Stanford, Ann Folwell. "More Than Just Words: Women's Poetry and Resistance at Cook County Jail." *Feminist Studies*, vol. 30, no. 2, 2004, pp. 277–301.

Stevenson, Bryan. *Just Mercy: A Story of Justice and Redemption*. Spiegel and Grau, 2015.

Stuckey, J. Elspeth. *The Violence of Literacy*. Boynton/Cook, 1991.

Sullivan, William M. *Work and Integrity: The Crisis and Promise of Professionalism in America*. HarperBusiness, 1995.

Tannenbaum, Judith. *Disguised as a Poem: My Years Teaching Poetry at San Quentin*. Northeastern UP, 2000.

Tannenbaum, Judith, and Spoon Jackson. *By Heart: Poetry, Prison, and Two Lives*. New Village Press, 2010.

Thoreau, Henry David. *Walden*. Empire Books, 2012.

Todd, Zoe. "An Indigenous Feminist's Take on the Ontological Turn: 'Ontology' Is Just Another Word for Colonialism." *Journal of Historical Sociology*, vol. 29, no. 1, 2016, pp. 4–22.

Tomlinson, Barbara, and George Lipsitz. "American Studies as Accompaniment." *American Quarterly*, vol. 65, no. 1, 2013, pp. 1–30.

Tuan, Yi-Fu. *Space and Place: The Perspective of Experience*. U of Minnesota P, 1977.

Tuck, Eve, and K. Wayne Yang. "Decolonization Is Not a Metaphor." *Decolonization: Indigeneity, Education & Society*, vol. 1, no. 1, 2012, pp. 1–40.

Verney, Marilyn Notah. "On Authenticity." *American Indian Thought*, edited by Anne Waters, Blackwell, 2004, pp. 133–39.

Villanueva, Victor, Jr.. *Bootstraps: From an American Academic of Color*. National Council of Teachers of English, 1993.

———, editor. *Cross-Talk in Comp Theory: A Reader*. 1st ed., National Council of Teachers of English, 1997.

———. "Hegemony: From an Organically Grown Intellectual." *Pre-Text: A Journal of Rhetorical Theory*, vol. 13, no. 1-2, 1992, pp. 17–34.

———. "Maybe a Colony: And Still Another Critique of the Comp Community." *JAC: A Journal of Composition Theory*, vol. 17, no. 2, 1997, pp. 183–90.

———. "Of Ideologies, Economies, and Cultures: Three Meditations on the Arizona Border." *Present Tense*, vol. 1, no. 2, 2011, pp. 1–5.

———. "On the Rhetoric and Precedents of Racism." *College Composition and Communication*, vol. 50, no. 4, 1999, pp. 645–61.

———. "Rhetoric, Racism, and the Remaking of Knowledge-Making in Composition." *The Changing of Knowledge in Composition: Contemporary Perspectives*, edited by Lance Massey and Richard Gebhardt, Utah State UP, 2011, pp. 121–33.

Vizenor, Gerald. *Griever: An American Monkey King in China*. Illinois State University, 1987.

———. *Manifest Manners: Postindian Warriors of Survivance*. Wesleyan UP, 1994.

————. *Narrative Chance: Postmodern Discourse on Native American Indian Literatures.* U of New Mexico P, 1989.

————, editor. *Survivance: Narratives of Native Presence.* U of Nebraska P, 2008.

————. "Trickster Discourse." *American Indian Quarterly,* vol. 14, no. 3, 1990, pp. 277–87.

————. *The Trickster of Liberty: Tribal Heirs to a Wild Baronage.* U of Minnesota P, 1988.

Waters, Anne, editor. *American Indian Thought.* Blackwell, 2004.

Weaver, Jace. *Other Words: American Indian Literature, Law, and Culture.* U of Oklahoma P, 2001.

Weber-Pillwax, Cora. "Indigenous Research Methodology: Exploratory Discussion of an Elusive Subject." *Journal of Educational Thought,* vol. 33, no. 1, 1999, pp. 31–45.

Weisser, Christian R. *Moving beyond Academic Discourse: Composition Studies and the Public Sphere.* Southern Illinois UP, 2002.

Wenger, Etienne. *Communities of Practice: Learning, Meaning, and Identity.* Cambridge UP, 1999.

Wenzer, Michel, director. *At Night I Fly.* Story AB, 2011.

Williams, Marty. "Life Without." *Too Cruel, Not Unusual Enough,* edited by Kenneth Hartman, The Other Death Penalty Project, 2013, pp. 107–14.

Williams, Rachel Marie-Crane. "Entering the Circle: The Praxis of Arts in Corrections." *The Journal of Arts Management, Law, and Society,* vol. 31, no. 4, 2002, pp. 293–303.

Wilson, Anita. "'I Go to Get Away from the Cockroaches:' Educentricity and the Politics of Education in Prisons." *The Journal of Correctional Education,* vol. 58, no. 2, 2007, pp. 185–203.

Wilson, Shawn. *Research Is Ceremony: Indigenous Research Methods.* Fernwood, 2008.

Wiltse, Ed. "Doing Time in College: Student–Prisoner Reading Groups and the Object(s) of Literary Study." *Critical Survey,* vol. 23, no. 3, 2011, pp. 6–22.

Winant, Howard. *The New Politics of Race: Globalism, Difference, Justice.* U Of Minnesota P, 2004.

## INDEX

## AUTHOR

**Anna Plemons** is a clinical assistant professor at Washington State University-TriCities, where she teaches in the English and Digital Technology and Culture programs. Since 2009 she has also taught nonfiction narrative through the Arts in Corrections program at New Folsom Prison. She has published work related to prison education in *Teaching Artist Journal, Community Literacy Journal,* and the edited collections *Prison Pedagogy: Learning and Teaching with Imprisoned Writers* (2018) and *Critical Perspectives on Teaching in Prison: Students and Instructors on Pedagogy Behind the Wall* (2019).

## BOOKS IN THE CCCC STUDIES IN WRITING & RHETORIC SERIES

*Beyond Progress in the Prison Classroom: Options and Opportunities*
Anna Plemons

*Rhetorics Elsewhere and Otherwise: Contested Modernities, Decolonial Visions*
Edited by Romeo García and Damián Baca

*Black Perspectives in Writing Program Administration: From the Margins to the Center*
Edited by Staci M. Perryman-Clark and Collin Lamont Craig

*Translanguaging outside the Academy: Negotiating Rhetoric and Healthcare in the Spanish Caribbean*
Rachel Bloom-Pojar

*Collaborative Learning as Democratic Practice: A History*
Mara Holt

*Reframing the Relational: A Pedagogical Ethic for Cross-Curricular Literacy Work*
Sandra L. Tarabochia

*Inside the Subject: A Theory of Identity for the Study of Writing*
Raúl Sánchez

*Genre of Power: Police Report Writers and Readers in the Justice System*
Leslie Seawright

*Assembling Composition*
Edited by Kathleen Blake Yancey and Stephen J. McElroy

*Public Pedagogy in Composition Studies*
Ashley J. Holmes

*From Boys to Men: Rhetorics of Emergent American Masculinity*
Leigh Ann Jones

*Freedom Writing: African American Civil Rights Literacy Activism, 1955–1967*
Rhea Estelle Lathan

*The Desire for Literacy: Writing in the Lives of Adult Learners*
Lauren Rosenberg

*On Multimodality: New Media in Composition Studies*
Jonathan Alexander and Jacqueline Rhodes

*Toward a New Rhetoric of Difference*
Stephanie L. Kerschbaum

*Rhetoric of Respect: Recognizing Change at a Community Writing Center*
Tiffany Rousculp

*After Pedagogy: The Experience of Teaching*
Paul Lynch

*Redesigning Composition for Multilingual Realities*
Jay Jordan

*Agency in the Age of Peer Production*
Quentin D. Vieregge, Kyle D. Stedman, Taylor Joy Mitchell, and Joseph M. Moxley

*Remixing Composition: A History of Multimodal Writing Pedagogy*
Jason Palmeri

*First Semester: Graduate Students, Teaching Writing, and the Challenge of Middle Ground*
Jessica Restaino

*Agents of Integration: Understanding Transfer as a Rhetorical Act*
Rebecca S. Nowacek

*Digital Griots: African American Rhetoric in a Multimedia Age*
Adam J. Banks

This book was typeset in Garamond and Frutiger by Barbara Frazier.
Typefaces used on the cover include Garamond and News Gothic.
The book was printed on 50-lb. White Offset paper
by Seaway Printing Company, Inc.